EUSTON STATION
THROUGH TIME
John Christopher

AMBERLEY PUBLISHING

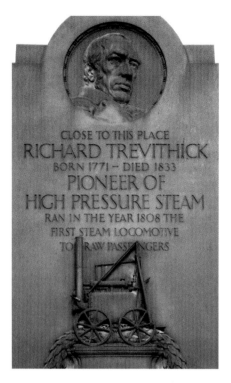

Left: This plaque in Gower Street commemorates Richard Trevithick's demonstration of his steam locomotive at Euston Square in 1809, an un-named green-field site at the time. However, there is no connection with the railway station being located near here.

About this book

The illustrations in this book encourage the reader to explore many aspects of Euston Station. They seek to document not only its history, its architecture and the changes that have occurred over the years, but also record the day-to-day life of this important railway terminus. Although Euston has suffered at the hands of the modernisers and developers, the station tells a fascinating story and there is much to be seen. Hopefully this book will encourage you to delve a little deeper when exploring Euston and its environs, but please note that public access and photography is sometimes restricted for reasons of safety and security.

First published 2012

Amberley Publishing
The Hill, Stroud
Gloucestershire, GL5 4EP

www.amberley-books.com

Copyright © John Christopher, 2012

The right of John Christopher to be identified as the Author of this work has been asserted in accordance with the Copyrights, Designs and Patents Act 1988.

ISBN 978 1 4456 0529 6

British Library Cataloguing in Publication Data.
A catalogue record for this book is available from the British Library.

Typeset in 9.5pt on 12pt Celeste.
Typesetting by Amberley Publishing.
Printed in the UK.

Introduction

Euston Station is unique. Not only was it the first London terminus for an inter-city railway when it opened in 1837, it also holds the dubious distinction of being the only one to have been entirely rebuilt. Several of London's other big termini were threatened with a similar fate at different times, but have survived moderately intact. The possible exceptions being Victoria Station, which has seen the loss of a major section of the London Brighton & South Coast Railway's train shed, and Charing Cross and Cannon Street which have undergone major refurbishments. Euston, however, is in a league of its own. The station's old train sheds – the platforms and covered areas – were workmanlike enough, but frankly, as pieces of architecture or engineering, they were unremarkable. Certainly they were not of the calibre of Isambard Kingdom Brunel's triple arches of iron and glass at Paddington, or the soaring single span of William Henry Barlow's St Pancras roof. The glory of the old Euston Station lay in its Great Hall and, most monumentally, the famous Doric arch that towered above the surrounding buildings. This had no practical function other than to proclaim that here was the future, the gateway to distant cities. It was a statement in stone that the railways had arrived and that they were here to stay. Unfortunately, by the 1960s such symbolism seemed irrelevant to Euston's custodians at the time, British Rail, and they gave us a new station in the 'international modern' style. One described variously as either 'imaginative and distinctive' or a 'dingy, grey, horizontal nothingness'.

Putting aside the architectural merits of the new structure, for now at least, this rebuilding means that the usual Through Time format of then-and-now pictures becomes irrelevant as there are precious few points of commonality. Accordingly, *Euston Station Through Time* is divided into distinct time periods covering the station's origins, the London & North Western Railway years, the LMS and concluding with the traumatic demolition and rebirth. Therefore it is more a case of then-and-then in the early stages, and only then-and-now later on or where appropriate. Ironically, if the HS2 high-speed rail link between London and Birmingham does go ahead, it may result in yet another reincarnation for Euston Station and a whole new chapter in this story.

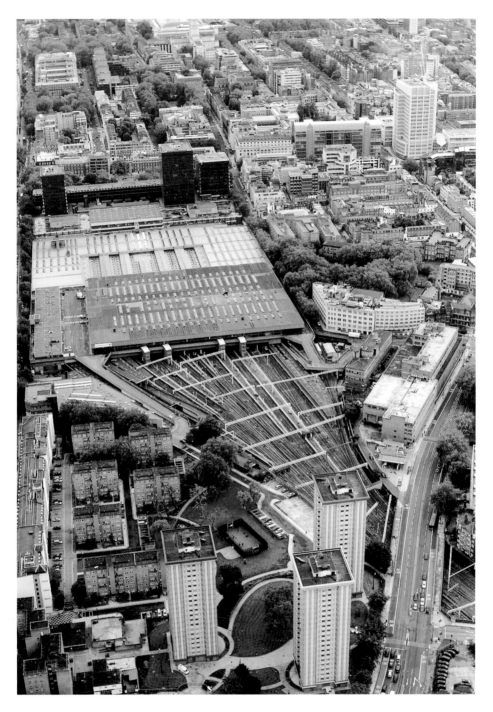

A recent aerial view of Euston Station, looking northwards. The large slab-like rectangle is the train shed roof with the higher flat roof of the main concourse on the far side and just before the darker office blocks. Euston Road runs left to right near the top of the photograph, and the LMS memorial in Euston Grove is visible beyond the offices. Euston House is just out of the frame to the left. The signal box building is on the right of the picture; note the access ramps leading to and from the Red Star parcel depot. (*Network Rail*)

The London & Birmingham Railway

When an Act of Parliament was passed in 1833 permitting the construction of the London & Birmingham Railway (L&BR), the original plan had been to terminate the line at Chalk Farm, roughly where the Camden Roundhouse stands and about a mile to the north of the present Euston site. It was the company's engineer, Robert Stephenson – the son of George Stephenson – who suggested extending the line further south to the edge of the city at the New Road, as Euston Road was known until 1857. Stephenson wanted to construct the terminus on the Kings Cross site, but facing severe opposition from landowners he opted instead for the site at Euston Grove. At one stage there were discussions with the Great Western Company concerning a sharing of facilities at Euston, but they fell through, partly because of the issue of incompatible gauges, and the GWR's engineer, Isambard Kingdom Brunel, went on to do his own thing at Paddington.

While Stephenson was responsible for planning the L&BR's station, the detailed design work was carried out by others. The train sheds were designed by Charles Fox (later Sir Charles), and the architectural frontispiece including the imposing Doric portico – technically a propylaeum as a portico is attached to a building – was the work of the celebrated architect Philip Hardwick. When the station opened in July 1837, the arch was still under construction and wouldn't be completed until May the following year. Behind the arch, the station consisted of the booking office and on its eastern side the departure and arrival platforms, corresponding with Platform 6 on the 1938 station plan shown on page 38. The platforms were 420 feet (128 m) long and covered for only half their length by the twin train shed roofs, which were supported on iron columns and arches. Each platform was served by two lines of track and these were linked via turntables.

Passengers catching a train would collect their numbered ticket from the booking office and then pass through to the departures platform, which was quaintly referred to as the Departure Parade. The original timetable listed six through trains to Birmingham on weekdays, two First Class, two Mails and two Mixed, and the journey time on the 112 mile (180 km) route was around five and a half hours. As can be seen from the illustration on page 8, the second class carriages had open sides and only the first class passengers had the benefit of enclosed compartments. The wealthy gentry had the option of having their own coaches conveyed on flat-bed wagons, and some compartments were convertible into sleeping-cars on the night Mail trains.

Although Euston Station was convenient for the railway travellers, its location at the bottom of a mile-long incline up to the Regents Canal and Chalk Farm was less than ideal from the engineer's point of view. Stephenson had concerns that the existing locomotives would not be able to haul heavily laden trains up the 1 in 70 gradient of the Camden Hill Incline and accordingly he devised a system which he termed the 'endless rope'. This involved a continuous cable which would be wound by stationary steam engines housed at the top of the hill. Departing trains would be man-handled out of the station and connected to the rope at the base of the incline and then pulled to the top of the hill, where they would be connected to locomotives. Communication between the staff at the bottom and the top of the hill was by means of 'mysterious moaning' conveyed by an atmospheric or talking tube. The Down trains arriving from Birmingham would be unhitched at Chalk Farm and their descent would be in the hands of men known as 'bank-riders' who operated the brakes. This cumbersome operation continued until 1844, by which time the newer locomotives were considered to be sufficiently powerful, and it explains why no locos are shown in the early images of the station.

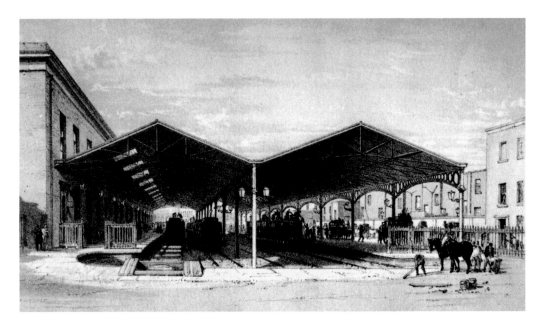

The newly-opened Euston Station in 1838 showing the twin-roofed train shed. The 'Departures Parade' is on the west side, shown on the left, and newly arrived passengers are disembarking on the right where their carriages are waiting. The L&BR's station offices are in the simple two-storey building on the left.

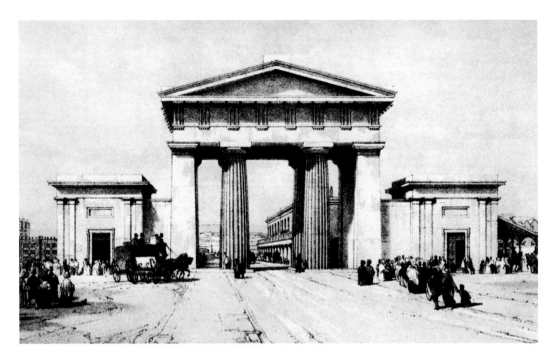

A gateway to the new railway

The artist J. C. Bourne depicted the Euston Arch as a classically-inspired and monumental structure standing in a romanticised setting uncluttered by other buildings. The two-storey station building can be glimpsed through the archway, and the train shed is to the far right. In the later view below, a postcard from around 1905, the newer station buildings from the 1870s expansion are evident, and the arch – strictly speaking a propylaeum – has been inscribed with the name of the station.

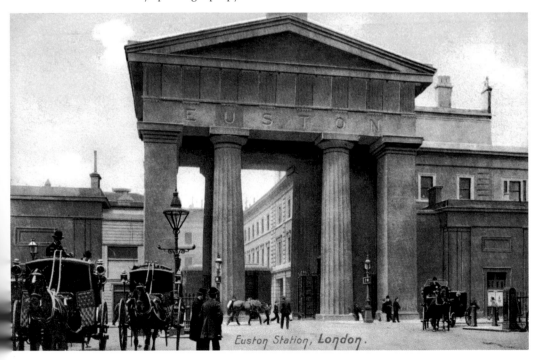

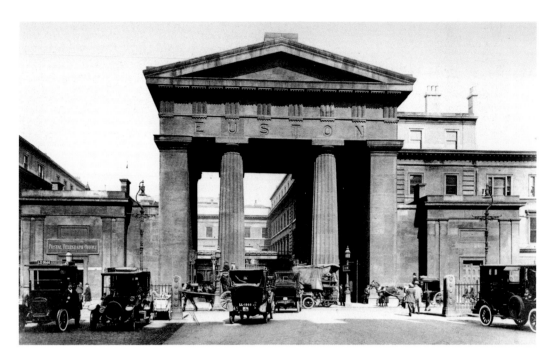

The Euston Arch

Slightly grimier but basically unchanged, this photograph from *c.* 1910 gives a truthful impression of the arch's huge size. Designed by Philip Hardwick, it stood 72 feet high. A narrow spiral staircase led to windowless offices within the pediment itself, and the square lodges to either side were also utilised. The one on the left bears a sign for the Postal Telegraph Office. These decorative iron casts from the central entrance are now displayed at the National Railway Museum in York.

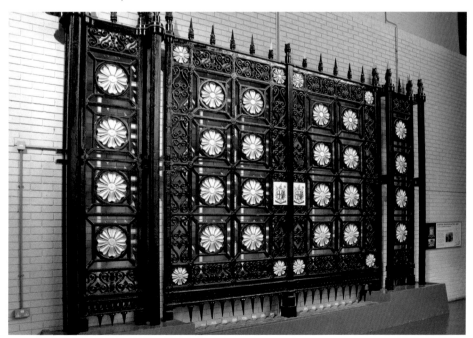

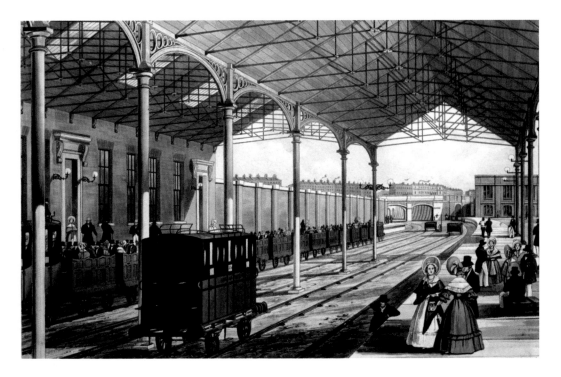

The original train shed

When Euston opened in 1838, the departure and arrivals platforms were each served by two lines of track. Most of the carriages or coaches are shown as being open topped, and note the absence of locomotives – see page 11. These platforms correspond to Platforms 7 and 6 in the later photograph, with the iron roof supports and columns still in place, albeit extended for greater height.

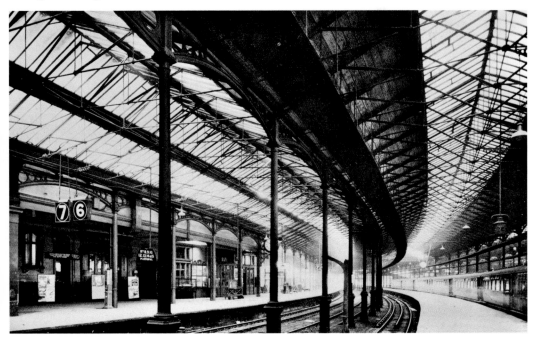

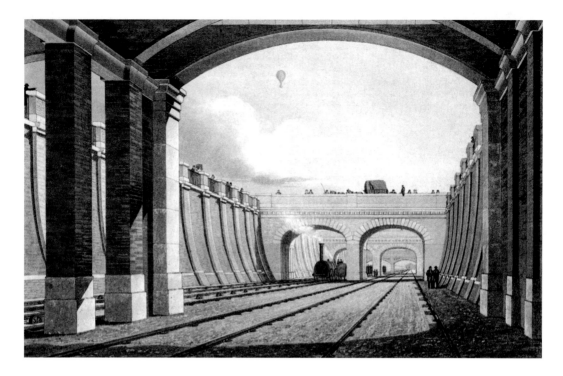

Cuttings

The L&BR cutting, above, is a finely proportioned piece of architecture in comparison with today's equivalent. Unfortunately we have lost something along the way as the railways grew ever bigger. Looking north from Euston, the view is dominated by a forest of gantries and overhead cables. This London Overground Class 378 EMU – for Electrical Multiple Unit – is arriving on a suburban service in 2012. The signal box building is to the left.

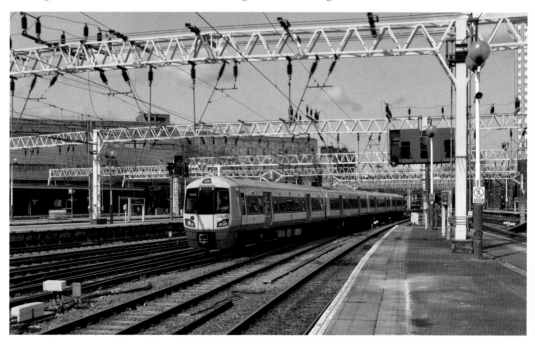

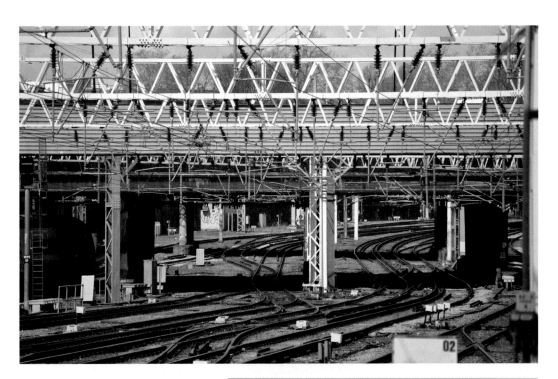

Stephenson's 'endless rope'

Fearing that the existing locomotives might struggle to haul trains up the Camden Hill Incline, a stationery winding engine was installed in an underground engine house on the far side of the Regents Canal. Trains departing from Euston were attached to a continuous rope which was pulled up the hill by the steam-driven engine built by the Maudslay engineering company. Downward trains were controlled by 'bank-riders' who rode on the carriages and operated the brakes. This system remained in use until 1844. The stationery engine and tall chimney stacks for the boilers have long gone, but the underground chambers still remain.

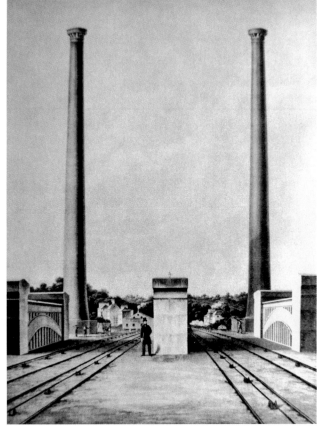

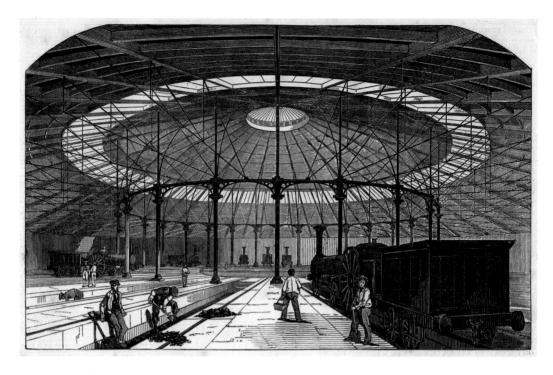

Camden Goods Depot and Roundhouse

A 30-acre triangle of land at the top of Camden Hill, situated between Chalk Farm Road and the Regents Canal, was established by the L&BR as the Camden Goods Depot in 1839. The Great Circular Engine House was completed in 1847 and, with a diameter of 160 feet, it could originally house up to twenty-four locomotives around a central turntable. In the 1960s it was converted into the Roundhouse concert venue.

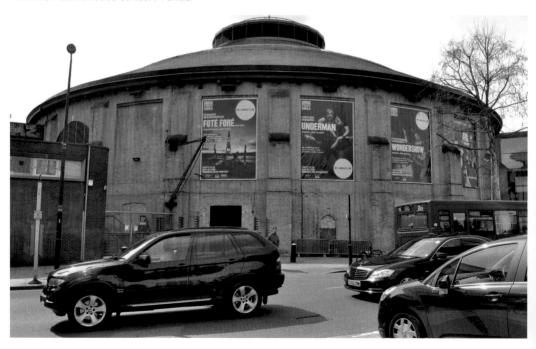

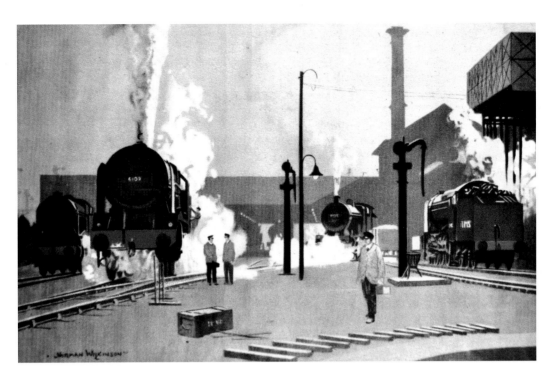

Camden Depot

The Camden Depot expanded very quickly and in this 1935 poster by Norman Wilkinson several LMS locos are shown being readied in front of the Camden Engine Sheds. A Morrisons supermarket occupies the site of the goods sheds, but many of the other buildings have survived. This 2012 photograph shows the Interchange Warehouse seen from Camden Lock Place on the edge of Camden's famous market area.

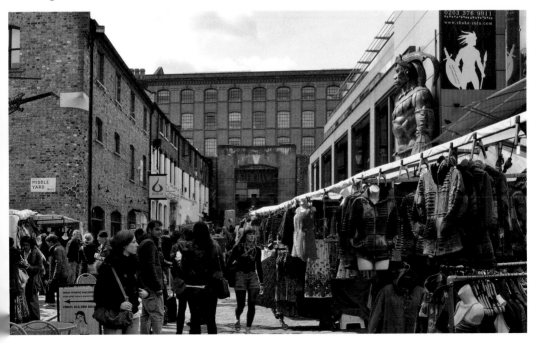

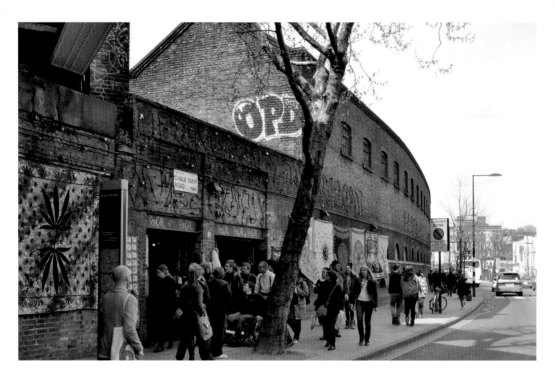

The Camden Stables

Up until the Second World War all of the railway companies relied heavily on horse power to move the goods, within the yard and to and from their customers' premises. At its peak some 700–800 horses worked at the Camden Goods Depot, and these stable blocks were built beside the Chalk Farm Road in the 1850s. Special horse tunnels were also constructed, passing underneath the tracks to provide access to the yards.

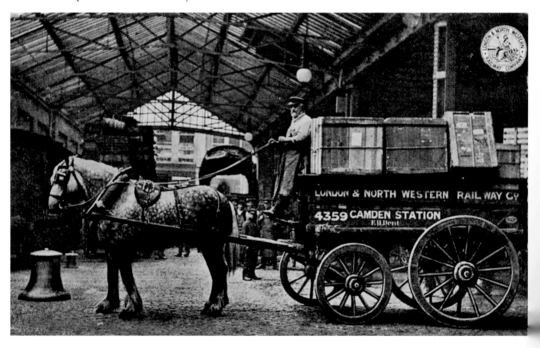

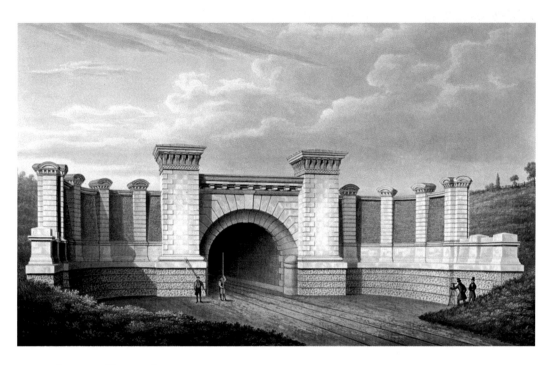

Primrose Hill Tunnel

Beyond the Camden Depot the main line curves to the west and enters the Primrose Hill Tunnel through the highly ornamental eastern portal. Completed in 1837, this was London's first railway tunnel and its main purpose was to placate Eton College, who owned the extensive Chalcot Estate. A second portal was added alongside in 1879, closely replicating the original one. The photograph below was taken in the 1930s, but today it is almost impossible to get a clear view of either portal.

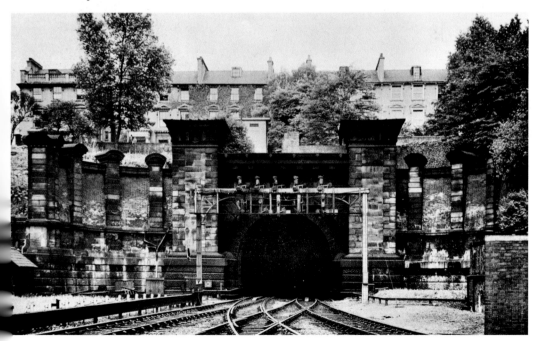

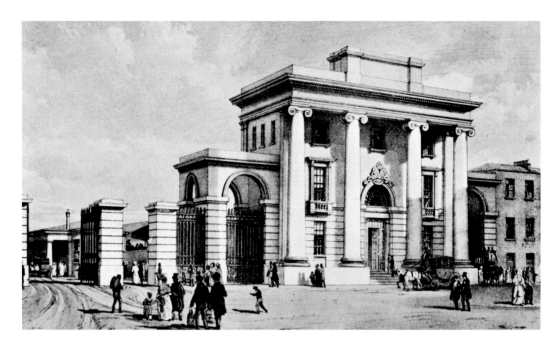

Birmingham's Curzon Street

Euston's arch was mirrored at the other end of the line. Opened in 1838 as the Birmingham Station, this was the terminus not only for the L&BR but also the Grand Junction Railway, with the companies having adjacent, parallel platforms. As with Euston, the entrance building was designed by Philip Hardwick and it features four columns under a flat-topped pediment. The two companies were merged within the LNWR in 1846 and when the more central New Street Station opened in 1854, they shared it with the Midland Railway. Accordingly, the regular passenger services to Curzon Street ceased, although some holiday excursion trains used the station until 1893. After that it continued as a goods station until its closure in 1966. (*Peter James*)

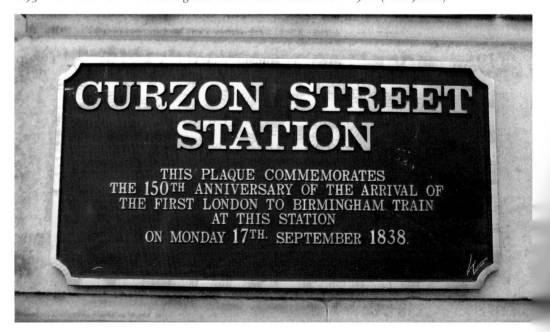

CURZON STREET STATION

THIS PLAQUE COMMEMORATES
THE 150TH ANNIVERSARY OF THE ARRIVAL OF
THE FIRST LONDON TO BIRMINGHAM TRAIN
AT THIS STATION
ON MONDAY 17TH. SEPTEMBER 1838.

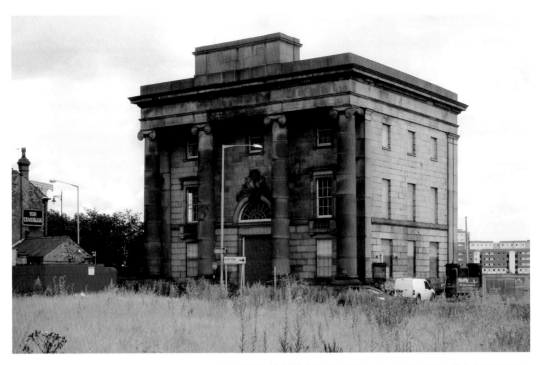

The comeback station

Unlike Euston, the Curzon Street Station has survived largely intact and it may yet enjoy a renaissance as the Birmingham terminus for the proposed HS2 high speed rail link (see page 82). Apparently, the two flanking entrance arches shown in J. C. Bourne's depiction of Curzon Street were part of the original design but never actually built. Appropriately enough, the coats of arms for both London and Birmingham are represented in the large decorative relief above the front door, but those cracks on the pillars will need some attention. (*Peter James*)

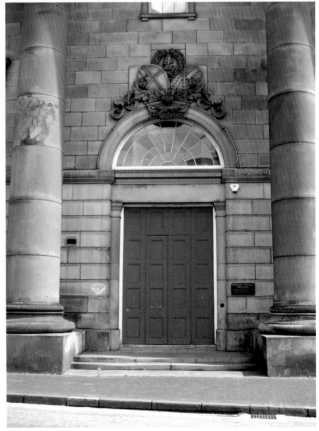

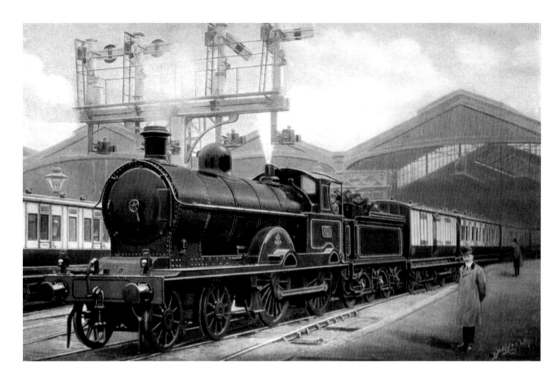

Mainline expresses

More than a hundred years apart, two wildly contrasting views of express trains about to depart from Euston Station on the West Coast Main Line route. Above, an LNWR locomotive *c.* 1905 and, below, the sleek nose of *Virgin Quest*, a Class 390 Pendolino EMU operated by Virgin Trains, photographed in 2012.

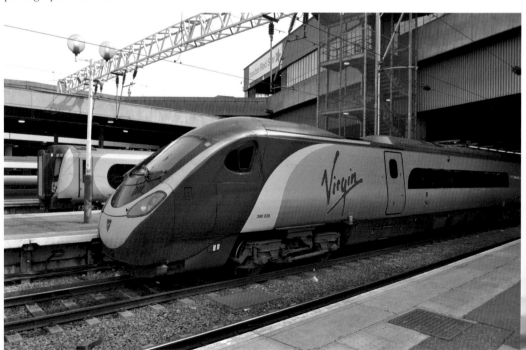

London & North Western Railway

The London & Birmingham Railway had a relatively short life. In 1846 it was amalgamated with two other companies, the Grand Junction and the Manchester & Birmingham, to form the London & North Western Railway (LNWR) with its headquarters at Euston. Over the ensuing decades the LNWR acquired a long list of other companies to become the largest in Britain. Its trains linked the cities of London, Birmingham, Manchester, Liverpool and Leeds. They pushed northwards into Scotland and, in cooperation with the Caledonian Railway, to both Edinburgh and Glasgow. They also handled the Irish Mail for the government between Euston and Holyhead, and they operated several steamships on the Irish Sea crossing.

The formation of the LNWR had been at the height of the railway mania of the 1840s and to meet the increase in traffic, Euston Station had to expand quickly. New buildings were added between the arch and the platforms, including the imposing Great Hall, which was over 125 feet (38 m) in length and 62 feet (19 m) from the floor to the elaborately corbelled and coffered ceiling. Opened in 1849, it was designed by Philip Charles Hardwick, the son of the architect who had bestowed the station with its imposing arch. Twin staircases curved up to the Shareholders' Meeting Room, and carved stone bas-reliefs in the high corners of the Great Hall celebrated the major cities linked by the railway. At the foot of the stairs stood E. H. Bailey's statue of George Stephenson, now on display in the National Railway Museum, York. Sir John Betjeman, who famously championed the cause of railway architecture, described the Great Hall as 'one of London's finest rooms'.

The station continued to grow rapidly and by the 1870s the site occupied upwards of ten acres. Additional platforms and service roads were constructed and Euston Grove was created to provide a formal approach linking the arch with the twin lodges on Euston Street. Over the next two decades further platforms were added on the western side, with the final four completed by 1892, after which no major alterations were made for another seventy years. Ironically, it was because Euston had been London's first railway terminus that the main development was carried out in such a piecemeal fashion. It never had the bold engineering train shed that epitomises so many of the city's great stations, and instead the emphasis had been placed on the magnificent but entirely ornamental Euston Arch and the opulence of the Great Hall. Quite possibly this is what left Euston vulnerable to the drive for modernity in the 1960s.

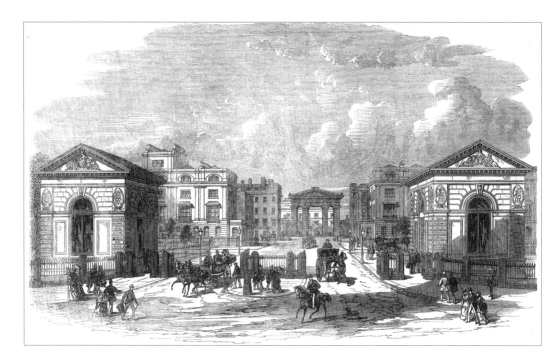

Station improvements

In 1869 the LNWR acquired the strip of land which separated the station entrance from Euston Road. A new drive, Euston Grove, was formed and the entrance flanked by two lodges at the Euston Road end, designed by J. B. Stansby. This created an unobstructed avenue leading to the arch, although it was slightly out of line, as can be seen on the plan on page 38. In this 1870 engraving from the *Illustrated London News* the arch is clearly more to the right, an alignment caused by the existing buildings on Drummond Street. In addition to the new entrance drive, the train shed roofs were raised by an additional 6 feet and the station enlarged on both sides.

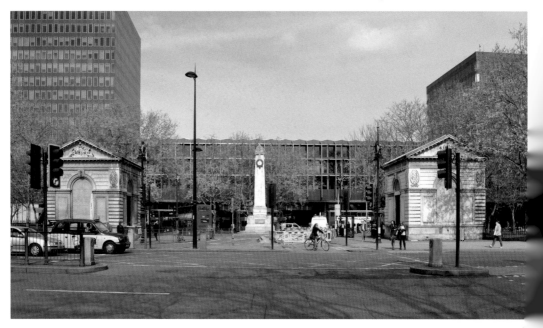

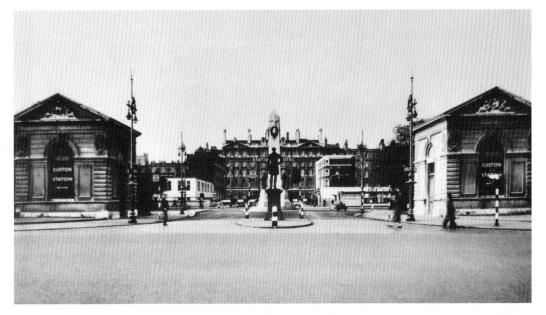

Euston Grove

The new entrance drive didn't stay uncluttered for long. This photograph, taken around 1960 shortly before the rebuild, shows the Euston Hotel spanning the road and blocking the view of the arch, the war memorial and a statue of George Stephenson. Not to be confused with the one of his father in the Great Hall, this bronze statue by the sculptor Baron Carlo Marochetti stands on a base of polished Aberdeen granite and was presented by the Institution of Civil Engineers in 1871. Following the rebuild, it now stands in the square directly in front of the new station (see page 26).

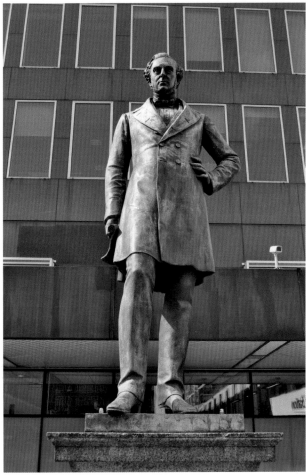

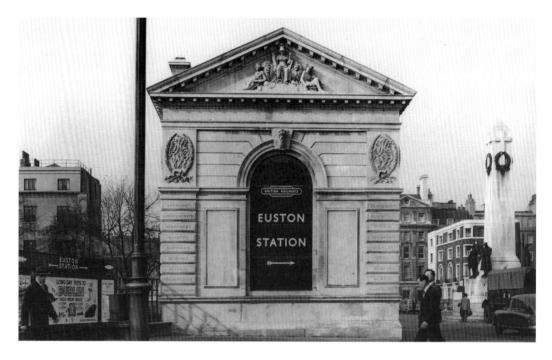

The Euston Road lodges

The two Portland stone lodges appear to be identical mirrors of each other, and in truth they are apart from the inscriptions on the corner stones. The west lodge, above, was originally used as an office for small parcels and enquiries, and is now a café. Note the LNWR monogram beneath the pediment on each corner. It is so intricate that the characters are lost in a tangle of fine carving.

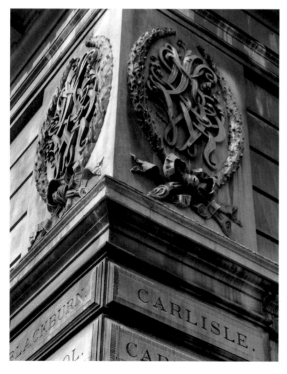

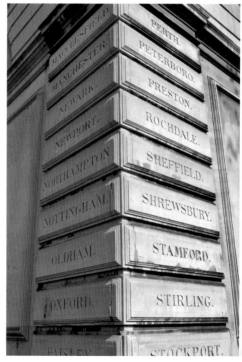

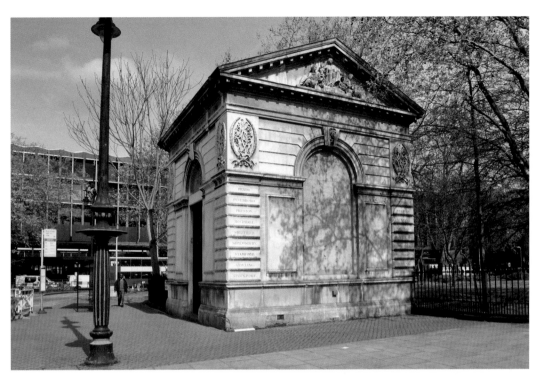

The eastern lodge appears to be unused at the moment. The 1870 engraving shows that the blank front panels were windows at one time, which makes sense if they were used as offices. Apart from the scale being somewhat exaggerated it is remarkably unchanged. The inscriptions are a list of the main towns and cities served by the LNWR presented in alphabetical order. The detail on the east lodge is shown opposite, with the names in this photograph running from Macclesfield to Stockport. The flash of red in the background indicates the location of the Euston Bus Station.

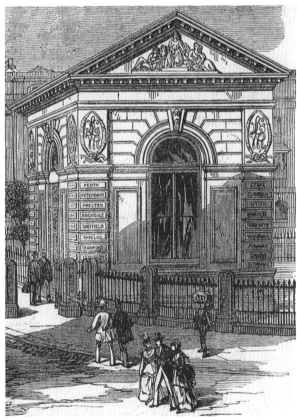

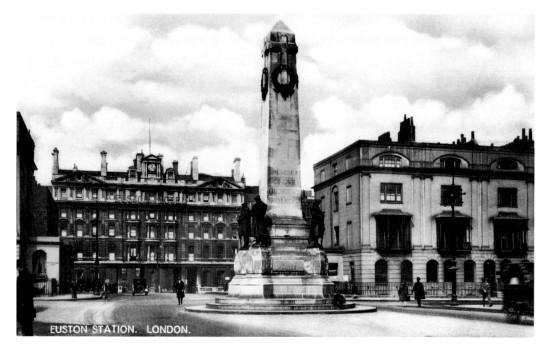

EUSTON STATION. LONDON.

LNWR War Memorial

Each of the railway companies lost members of staff in both World Wars. The LNWR War Memorial was designed by company architect R. Wynn Owen and unveiled by Earl Haig in October 1921 to commemorate the 3,719 employees who gave their lives in the First World War.

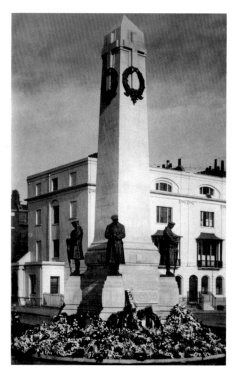

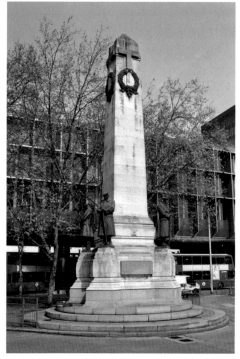

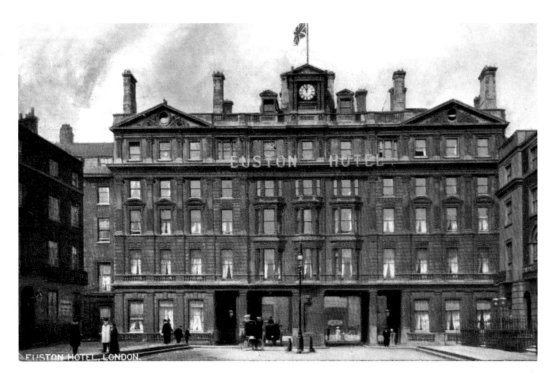

The Euston Hotel

In the 1880s the Euston and Victoria hotels on either side of Euston Grove were linked by a new building which spanned the road and blocked the view to the arch – see the map on page 38. This became the Euston Hotel, although in the 1957 photograph on page 21 it is signed as the Station Hotel. Its modern equivalent is the Euston Bus Station, shown below.

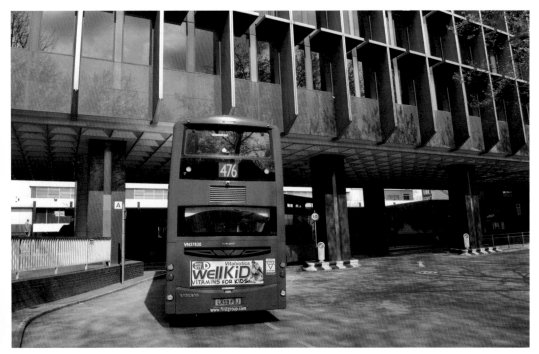

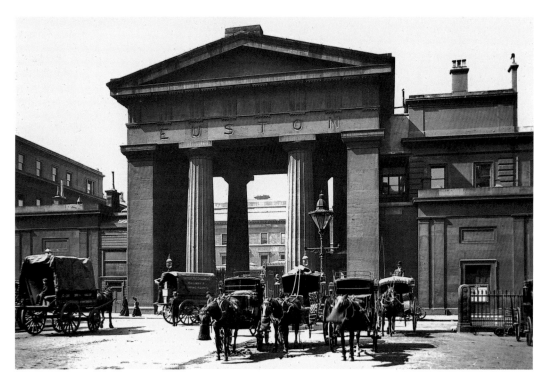

What a difference a hundred years or so can make

When the upper picture was taken, sometime in the 1890s judging by the absence of cars, the Euston Arch was a symbol of the railway's confidence and permanence. Few could have imagined the changes that would come in the new century when the LNWR was absorbed into the LMS, which in turn became a part of British Railways, and the arch was swept away because it was too expensive to move.

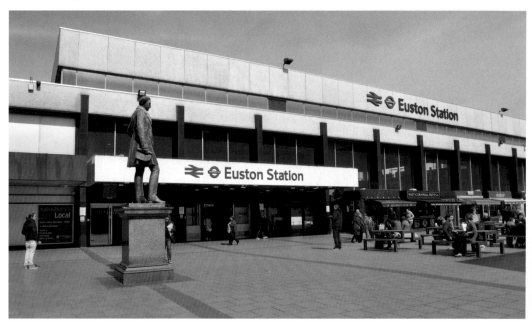

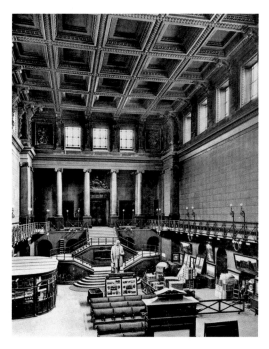
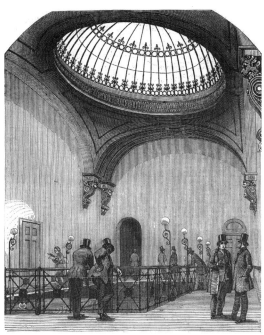

Relics of the Great Hall

Few relics have survived from Euston's Great Hall, designed by the younger Philip Hardwicke. The 1852 statue of George Stephenson, carved in marble by Edward Hodges Baily, is at the National Railway Museum in York along with the station clock which had stood opposite it. Shown top right is the gallery of the Booking Office.

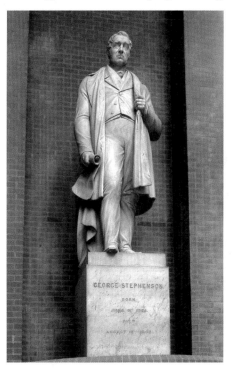
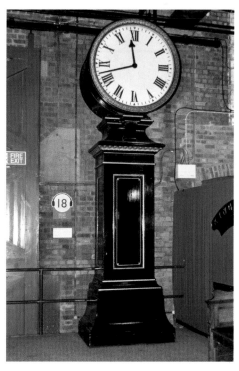

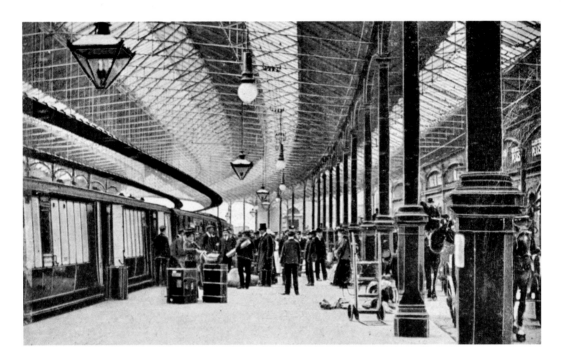

Euston platforms

On the eastern side of the station the platforms follow the gentle curves of the original 1838 layout, bending to the left as they leave the station. In these images, both taken from contemporary postcards, horse-drawn carriages and cabs wait on the platforms. The strips running above the trains were put there to protect the relatively low glass roof from being blasted by the locomotives' chimneys. LNWR trains were painted black and the coaches in 'spilt milk' white above a deep plum red.

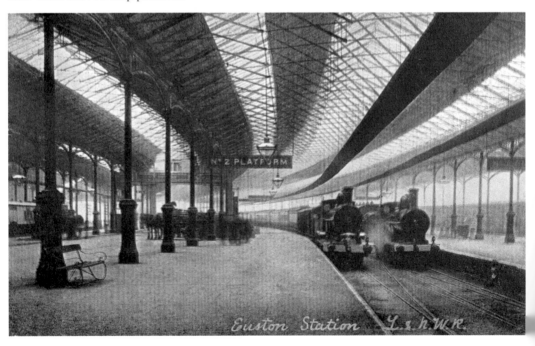

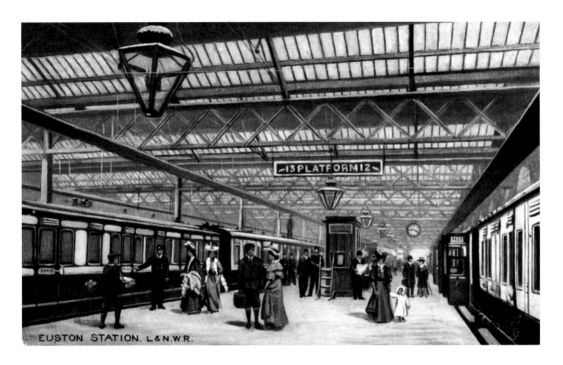

EUSTON STATION. L.& N.W.R.

Later platforms

The straight lines of the later LNWR platforms, in this case 12 and 13 shown above. The roof is of an uncomplicated ridge and furrow design, functional but unexceptional. The modern platforms at Euston – there are eighteen of them – have no direct correlation with the old numbers. Platforms 9 and 10, below, still have that slight curve to them.

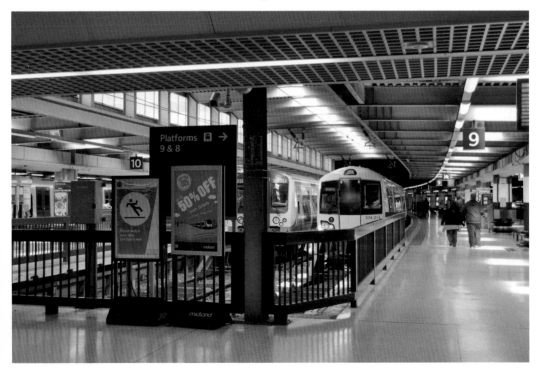

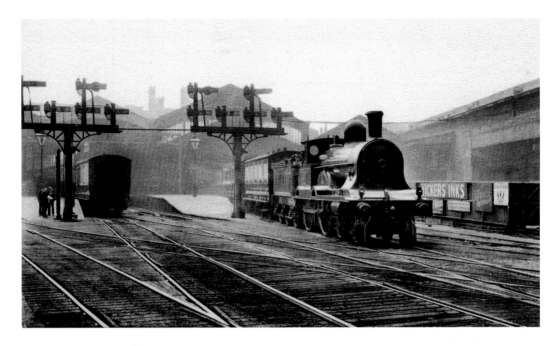

The American Special

Above, the 10.00 Scotch Express is departing from Euston. The locomotive appears to be of the same Dreadnought class as is shown in the photograph on page 32. These would have also hauled the LNWR's American Specials, a service commenced in 1898 to take wealthy passengers from Euston direct to Liverpool's Riverside Station. This was adjacent to the landing stages for the Cunard and White Star transatlantic liners. The American Specials were renowned for their high levels of comfort and service, and a dining saloon is shown below in this contemporary postcard. (*CMcC*)

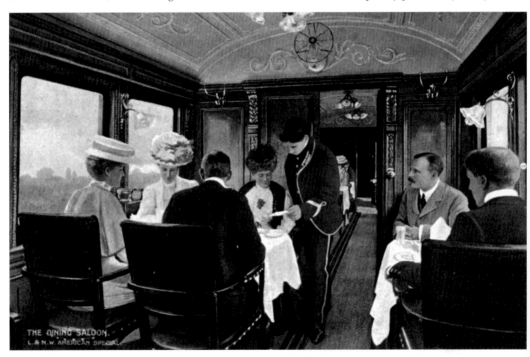

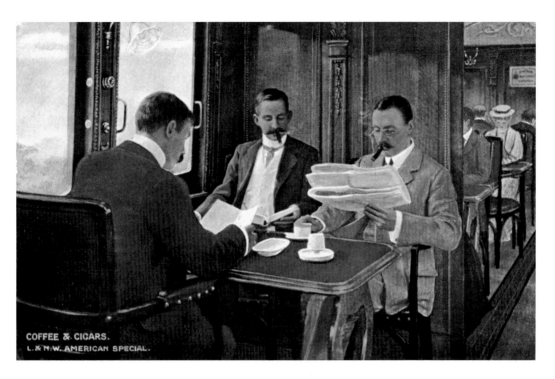

COFFEE & CIGARS.
L. & N.W. AMERICAN SPECIAL.

Coffee, cigars and newspapers for the men, or afternoon tea in the salon-de-luxe for the ladies. Note the free-standing chairs and furniture – Health and Safety would have had a field day on the American Specials. Liverpool Riverside was demolished in the early 1990s. (*CMcC*)

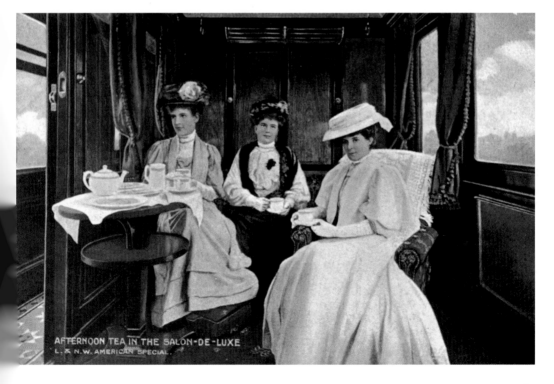

AFTERNOON TEA IN THE SALON-DE-LUXE
L. & N.W. AMERICAN SPECIAL.

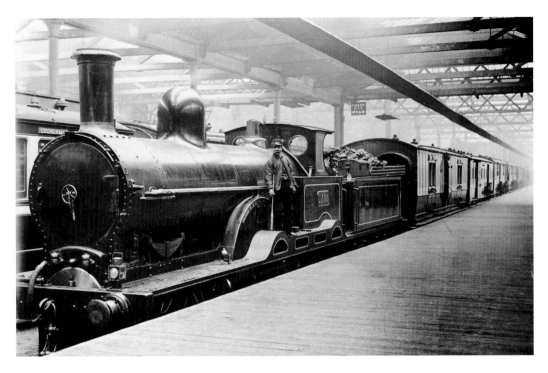

Archimedes and Virgin Quest
A wonderful photograph of No. 1395, *Archimedes*, of the LNWR's Dreadnought Class designed by
F. W. Webb. This locomotive was built at Crewe in 1886. The carriage in the background carries
a destination board for Manchester. (*LoC*) Below is the *Virgin Quest* Pendolino at Euston.

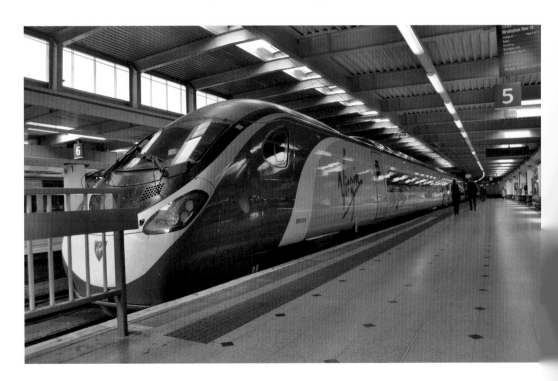

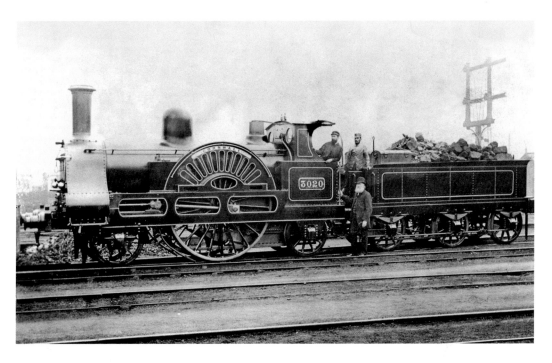

Cornwall

A rare example of a preserved early LNWR loco – most were absorbed into the LMS stock. Designed by Francis Trevithick, the son of Richard, *Cornwall* has a pair of 8 foot 6 inch driving wheels. Built at Crewe in 1847, it hauled express passenger trains on the West Coast Main Line until 1905 and is now displayed at the NRM's facility at Shildon in County Durham.

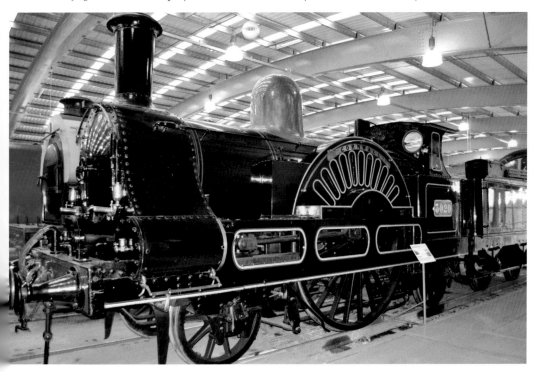

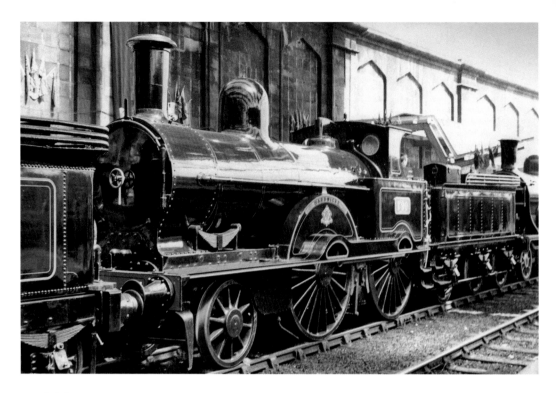

Hardwicke

Built in 1873, *Hardwicke* is a 2-4-0 of the Improved Precedent Class designed by F. W. Webb. In 1895, this locomotive set a new speed record during a period of intense rivalry with the GNR – known as the 'Race to the North' – when it covered the 141 miles between Crewe and Carlisle in 2 hours 6 minutes. Withdrawn in 1932, it is now an exhibit at the NRM in York.

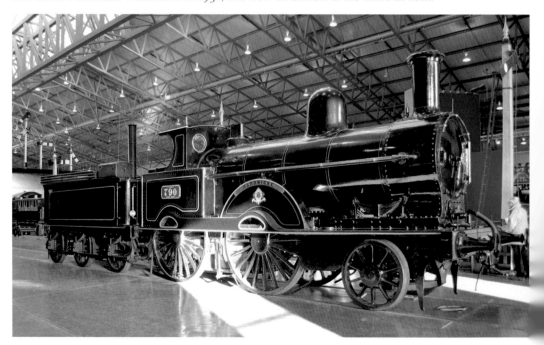

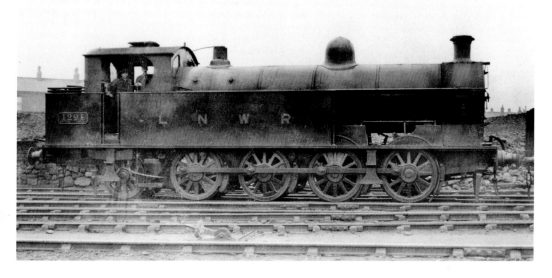

LNWR legacy

No. 1291 is an example of a later LNWR locomotive, a nameless hard-working Class 1185 0-8-2T built in 1917. It was re-numbered by the LMS as 7893 and finally withdrawn in 1934. At the other end of the spectrum is the LNWR's 1903 carriage for Queen Alexandra, the wife of Edward VII. This contemporary LNWR postcard shows the opulent Day Compartment. The carriage is also at the NRM, York.

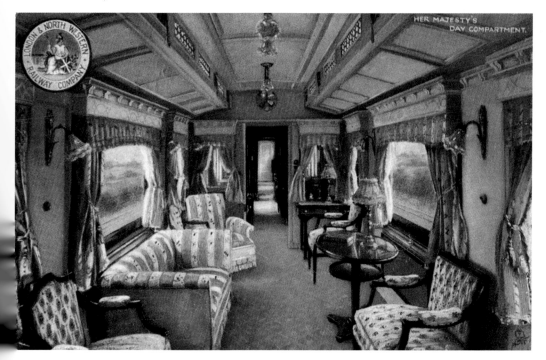

Formed as part of the regrouping of the railways in 1923, the London Midland & Scottish Railway had the largest territory of any of the 'Big Four'. It was the only company to operate trains in England, Scotland as well as parts of Northern Ireland and Wales. (*NTU*)

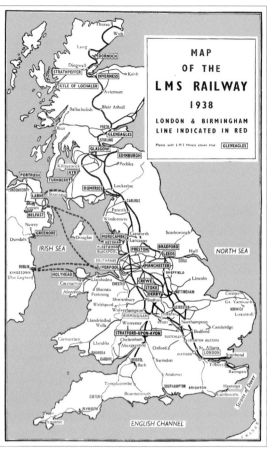

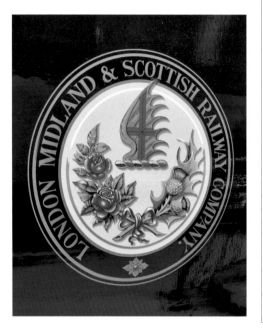

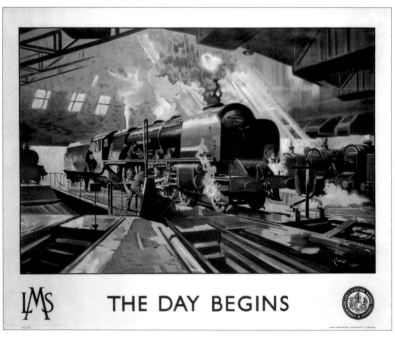

The LMS Era

By the early twentieth century, Britain's Victorian railway system had become inefficient and unprofitable with a multitude of companies often operating routes in direct competition with each other. A big shake-up was needed and it came with the Railways Act of 1921. Also known as the Grouping Act, this reorganised the 120 individual companies into the 'Big Four': the Great Western Railway (GWR); the London & North Eastern Railway (LNER); the Southern Railway (SR); and the London Midland & Scottish Railway (LMS). When the Act came into effect on 1 January 1923, the biggest company was the LMS, formed from the LNWR, the Midland Railway and the Caledonian as well as a number of smaller railways. After the Post Office, the LMS was the country's biggest employer and by 1938 its territory incorporated almost 7,000 miles of track. It was the only one of the Big Four operating in England, Scotland, Wales and Northern Ireland.

The principal LMS routes were the West Coast Main Line and the Midlands Main Line. The company also ran the Irish Mail train from Euston to Holyhead, inherited from the LNWR, and in cooperation with the Southern Railway managed to stray across GWR territory as far as Bournemouth on the south coast. But it was on the route to Scotland that the LMS competed fiercely with the LNER's rival East Coast Main Line services. This culminated in the dramatic speed record-breaking runs of the streamliners with the LMS's *Coronation* pushing the record to 114 mph (183 km/h) in 1937, followed by the LNER's A4 class *Mallard* taking it to 126 mph (203 km/h) in 1938.

Organisationally, the LMS was something of an unwieldy monster with a wide geographical spread and the rival factions within its former main constituents, the LNWR and Midland Railway, vying for control. Euston Station remained as the company's headquarters and principal London terminus, although the LMS also had the former Midland terminus at St Pancras. Apart from the smart new office block, Euston House, erected on Seymour Street in 1933, Euston Station changed little under the management of the LMS. However, it should be noted that by the time of the London & Birmingham Railway's centenary celebrations in 1938 the LMS was considering a plan for reconstructing Euston on the 'most modern' lines. At the time, they claimed that this scheme would 'make Euston one of the finest stations in the country, worthy of its distinguished history and ranking among the world's greatest termini'. In the event, the Second World War, and the subsequent nationalisation of Britain's railways, scuppered the LMS's grandiose plans. But for the old Euston Station, the reprieve was only temporary.

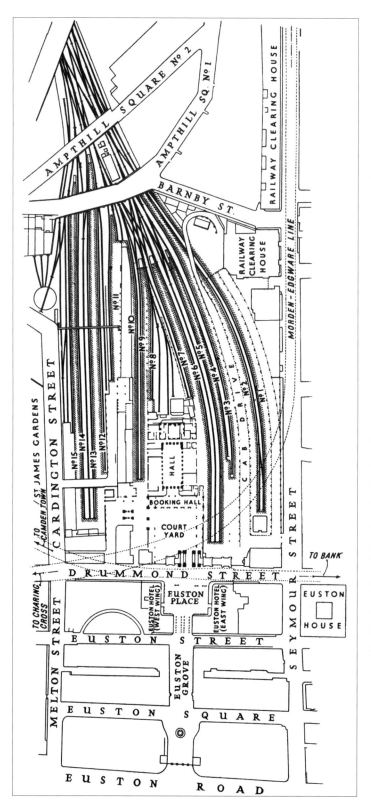

Euston Station, 1938
This plan, published on the station's centenary, reveals several layers of its history:

The original 1838 Departures and Arrivals Platforms correspond with Platform 6 on the plan, located to the right of the Booking Hall and Courtyard. The other platforms, on the west and east sides, were all added in the later nineteenth century station improvements.

The Euston Arch is just above the second 'D' in Drummond Street, and the Great Hall is shown in the centre, running north–south above the Booking Hall.

Moving southwards from Drummond Street, you find Euston Place and the Euston Hotel bridging Euston Grove. Continuing south on Euston Grove itself, the small circle represents the LNWR War Memorial, and beneath that are the gates and twin lodges on to Euston Road.

Note also Euston House on Seymour Street, and the Cab Drive running up between Platforms 2 and 3.

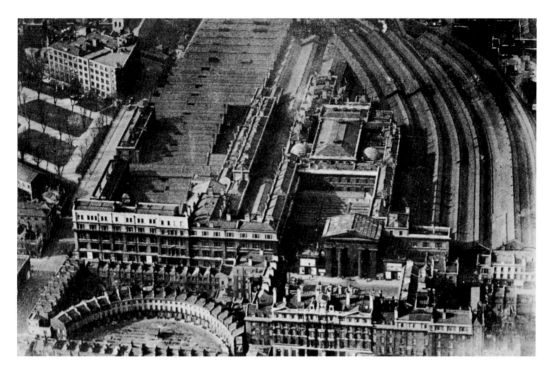

This 1930s aerial photo, facing northwards, helps to identify the various parts of the station, including the Euston Arch towering above Drummond Street. Platform 7 is shown below in this 1930s photo.

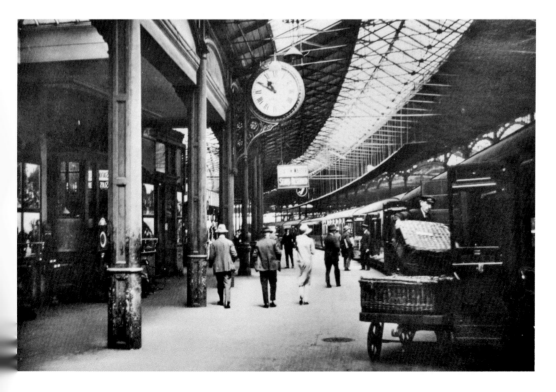

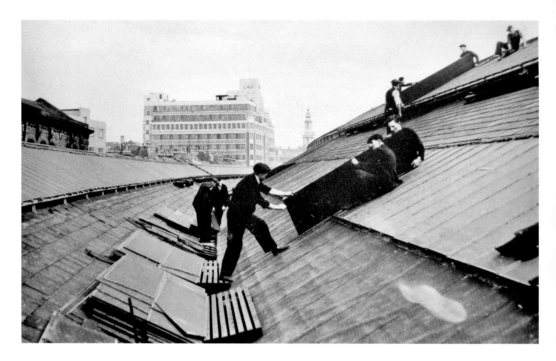

Euston House

In 1933 the LMS built itself a fine steel-framed office block in the Art-Deco influenced Moderne style. It is shown above, in the distance behind the men who are working to remove the glass on the train shed roof as a wartime precaution. It also features prominently in this fine marquetry panel produced to mark the railway's centenary in 1938. The large wooden panel was originally displayed in the station and is now at the NRM in York. Opposite, three views of Euston House looking as good today as when it was built.

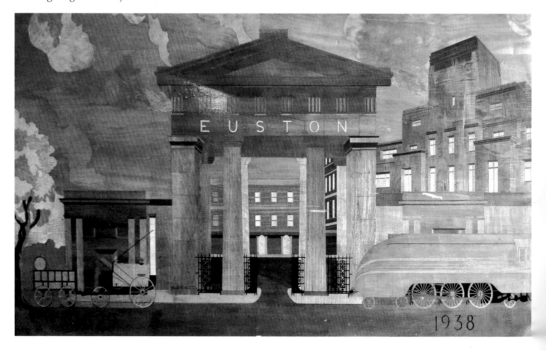

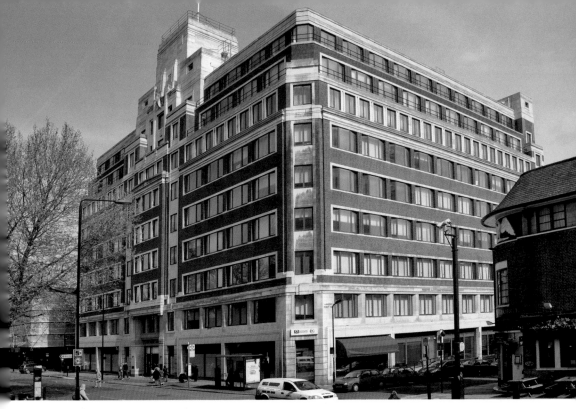

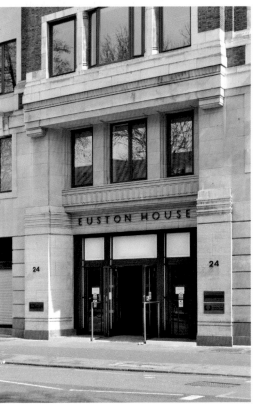

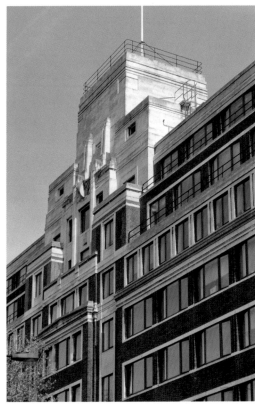

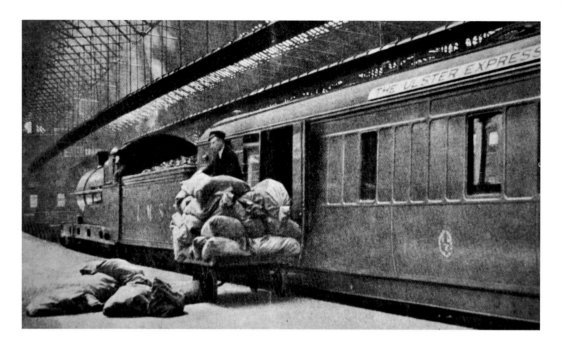

Busy platforms scenes from the LMS era: Above, a porter unloads mail bags delivered by the Ulster Express. The contract to carry the Irish Mail was a very important one for the company. Below, a special constable from the Railway Police oversees the loading of a van at Euston.

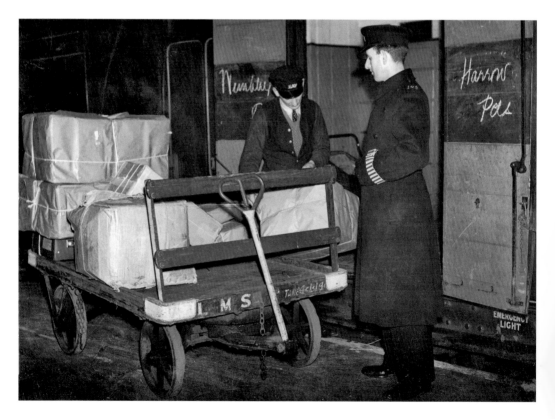

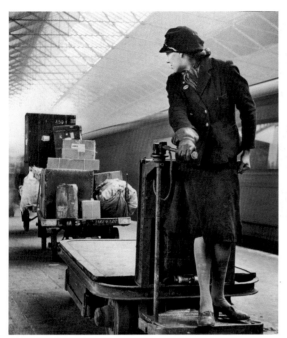
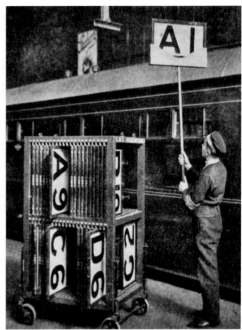

Above left: A female member of staff transports parcels and packages on a Greenwood & Batley electric battery-powered truck. Note her wonderfully wrinkly stockings. Right: A porter holds up a board displaying reserved seat numbers for passengers. Below: The only sort of platform traffic seen at Euston nowadays.

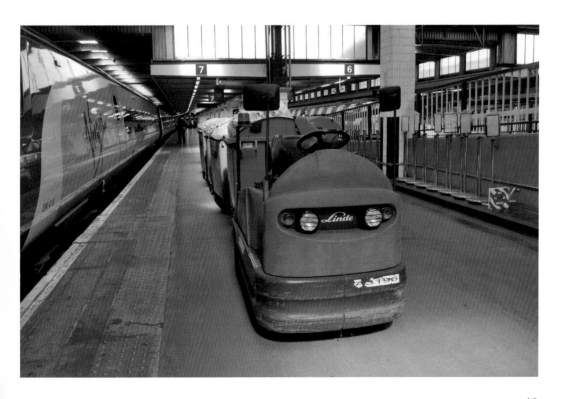

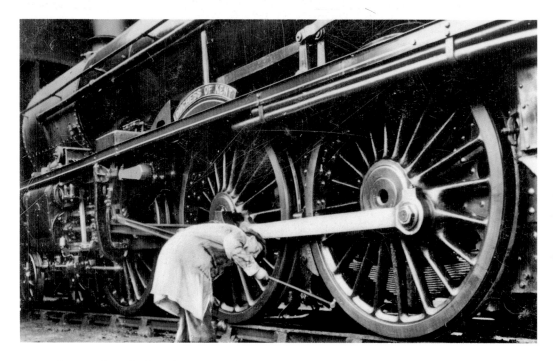

Doing the rounds with the Princess Royal Class

This LMS wheel tapper is literally sounding out the giant driving wheels, listening for the sound of any faults. This is No. 46212, the *Duchess of Kent*, which was built in 1935 and withdrawn in 1961. Below, No. 6208 *Princess Helena Victoria* is taking a spin on the turntable at the Camden sheds, turning by its own steam power. The vacuum brake pipe has been attached to one from the turntable. Both locos are of the Stanier Pacific Princess Royal Class used to haul the Royal Scot.

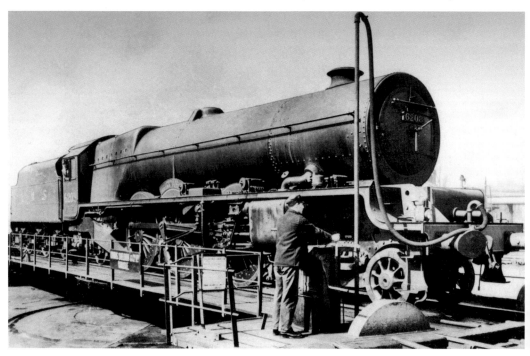

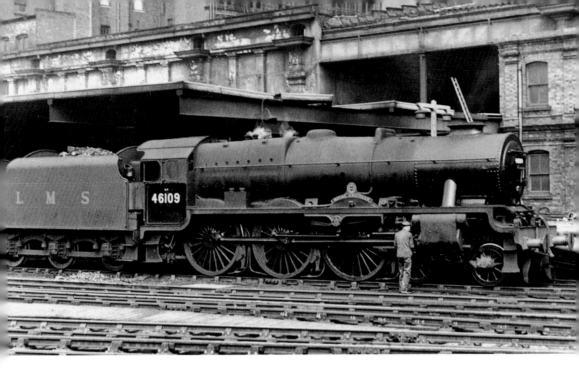

Royal Scot Class locomotives

No. 46109 is the *Royal Engineer*, a 4-6-0 express passenger locomotive of the LMS Royal Scot Class which was first introduced in 1927 specifically for the West Coast Main Line service out of Euston. Seventy were produced and No. 6126, shown below, is another of the same class. It was originally named *Sans Pareil*, a reference to an earlier locomotive which took part in the 1829 Rainhill Trials, but this was later changed to *Royal Army Service Corps*. The Royal Scot Class locos were substantially rebuilt between 1944 and 1955, and most acquired similar military-related names.

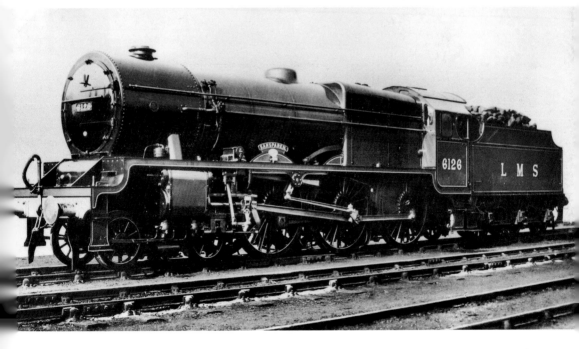

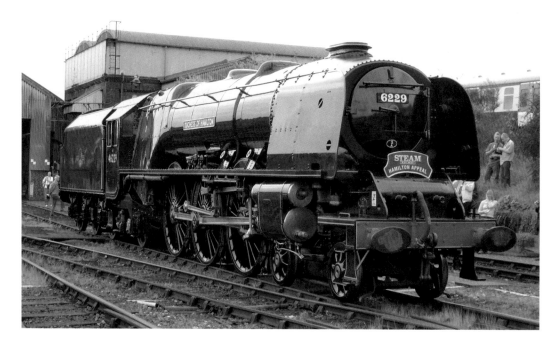

Coronation Class

The LMS Coronation Class was a bigger version of the company's Princess Royal Class. No. 6229, *Duchess of Hamilton*, was originally fitted with the rounded 'upturned-bathtub' streamline casing and go-faster stripes. This was removed in 1947, but has since been reinstated for the loco's display at the NRM (see page 49). (*Tivedshambo*)

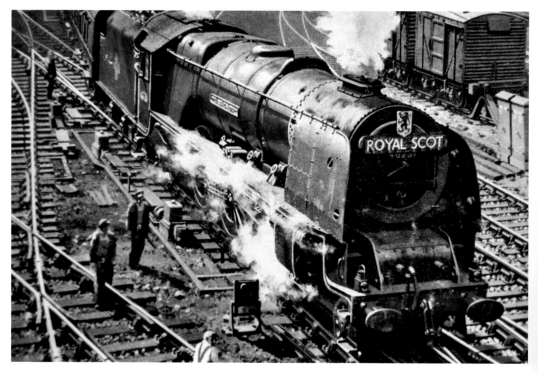

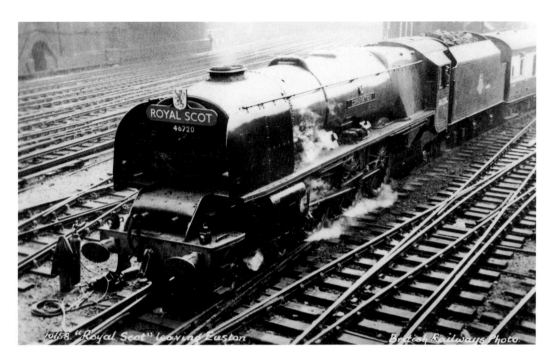

10158. "Royal Scot" leaving Euston   British Railways Photo.

The Coronation Scot

The eponymous *Coronation*, shown above in later BR livery and 46220 number, began life with streamlining finished in Caledonian Railway blue. In this form it set a new speed record of 114 mph, on the Euston to Glasgow run, in June 1937. The streamlined panels were removed in 1946 and the smoke deflectors were added. This LMS photograph, below, shows the construction of one of the Coronation Class locos at the Crewe works.

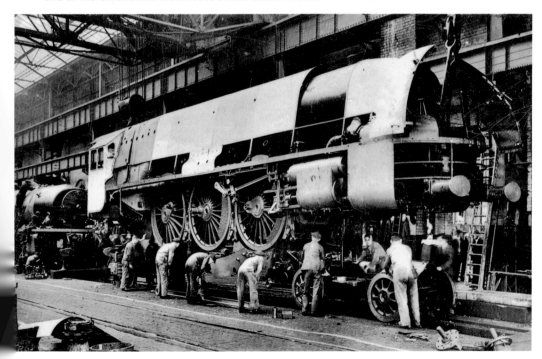

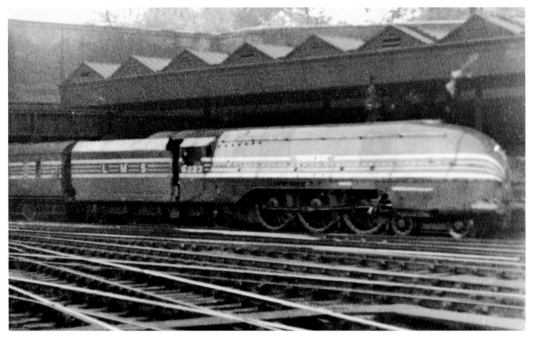

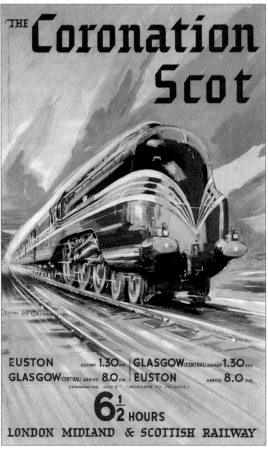

The streamliners

Introduced in 1937, the Coronation Class streamlined locos represented the modern face of the LMS. These were locos which could match the best of the LNER's and they also looked good on the company's publicity posters. No. 6223, *Princess Alice*, is shown at Euston in its original Caledonian Railway blue livery. Their main role was to haul the Coronation Scot on the West Coast Main Line and this 1937 poster by artist Bryan de Grineau promotes the 6½ hours run between Euston and Glasgow. (*CMcC, NTU*)

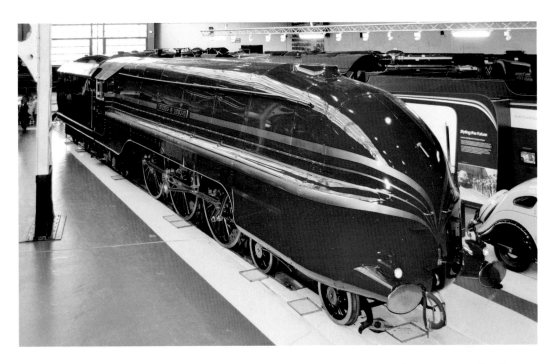

The re-streamlined *Duchess of Hamilton* on display at the NRM in York (see page 46 for the non-streamlined manifestation). Below, this LMS photograph shows one of the original Coronation Scot Class in the original blue livery with silver stripes. This was later changed to the maroon and gold. The Royal Scot express trains consisted of nine carriages with accommodation for up to 232 passengers. Critics have suggested that the streamlining was largely for publicity purposes, but undeniably the *Duchess* looks absolutely stunning.

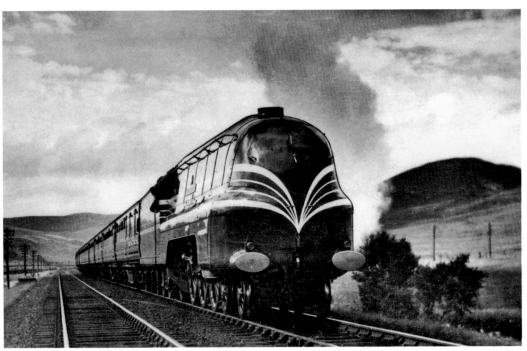

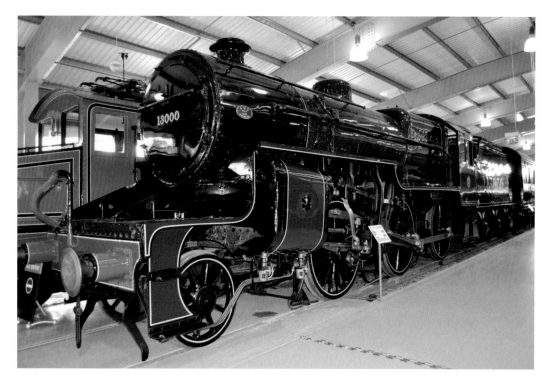

LMS Hughes Crab

After the streamliners we have the more workaday face of LMS locomotives. The 2-6-0 Hughes Crab Class was developed for mixed traffic. The un-named No. 13000 was built at Horwich in 1926 and is now preserved at the NRM's Shildon museum in Co. Durham, while 13229, below, is shown in service.

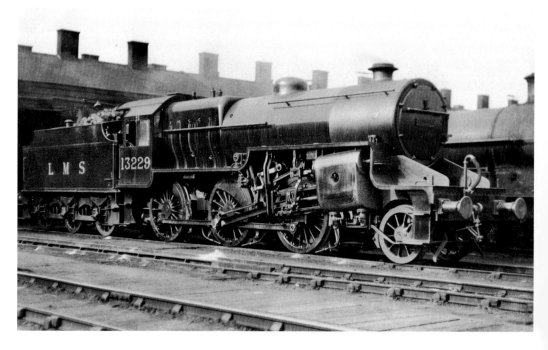

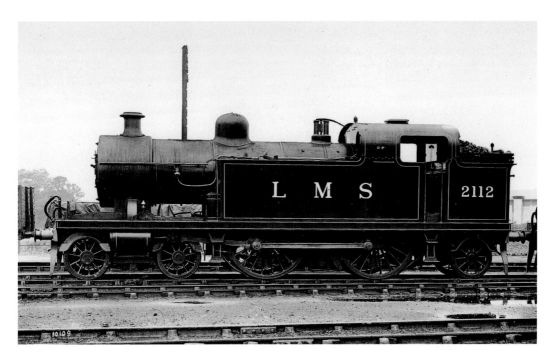

LMS tanks
No. 2112 was built in 1923. These 4-4-2T Class 3P-D locos were originally designed for the London Tilbury & Southend Railway. This particular example continued in service until 1952. No. 2500, below, is a Stanier-designed 2-6-4T. Built at the Derby works in 1934 and later absorbed into the British Rail stable, it was finally withdrawn in 1961.

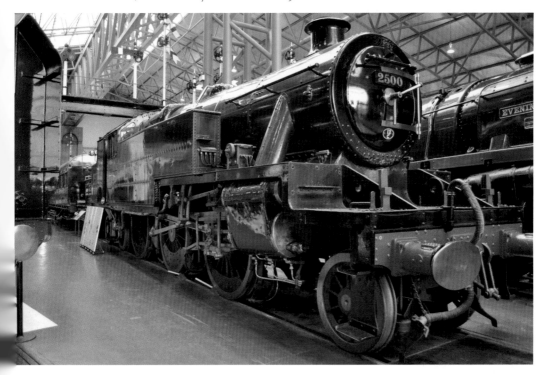

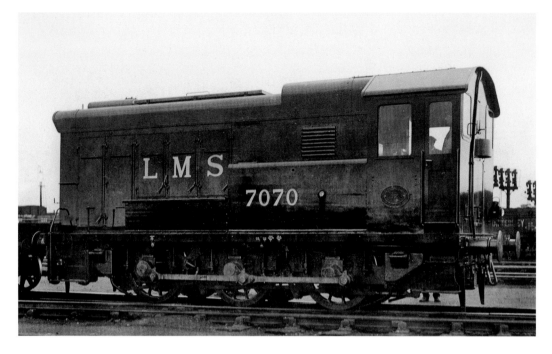

LMS diesels

No. 7070 is a pre-war 0-6-0 diesel electric shunter, built by the English Electric company in 1935. This design became the British Rail Class D3/6. On the other hand, the more compact No. 7050, below, is a one-off 0-4-0 design built at the Preston works in 1934. It is now preserved in the NRM collection in York.

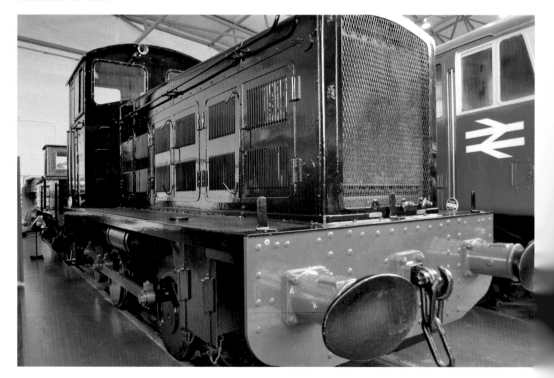

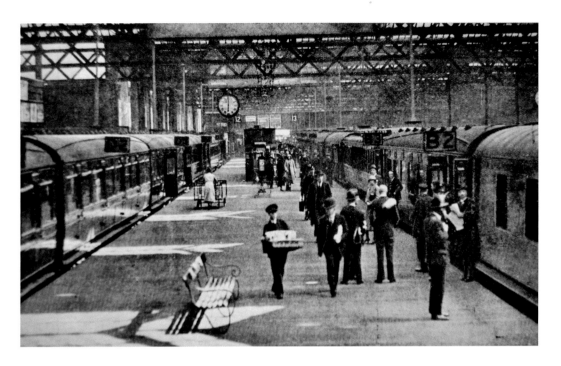

LMS coaches

This photograph of the Ulster Express, preparing to depart from Platform 13 on the Royal Mail service from London to Northern Ireland in the early 1930s, shows carriages in the post-grouping dark maroon livery adopted from the Midland Railway. 7965 is a four-wheeler Brake built in 1911 at the LNWR's Wolverhampton Works and later brought into LMS service. Finished with the distinctive yellow and black detailing, it is now at the Kent & Sussex Railway. (*Peter Skuse*)

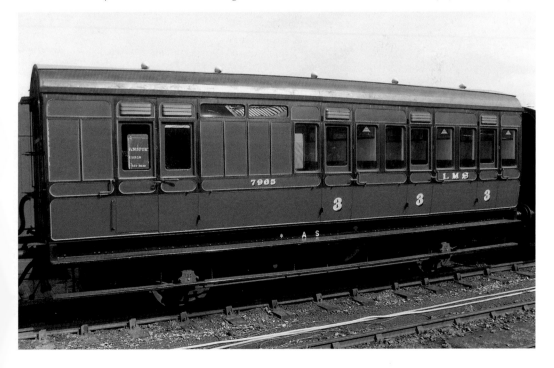

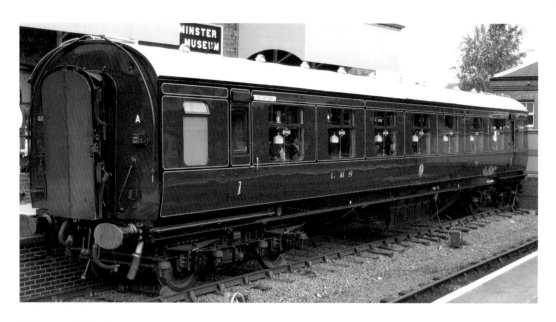

Dining and sleeping-cars

LMS 7511 is an Open First Class coach constructed at Wolverhampton in 1934. Intended for the express services, it could double-up as a dining car, as presented here at the Severn Valley Railway. (*Peter Skuse*) LMS Sleeping Car No. 14241 was built at Derby in 1928. Third Class sleeping accommodation was provided after an Act of Parliament permitted the railway companies to extend their sleeping accommodation. During the day it served as an ordinary Third Class carriage. It is displayed at the NRM, Shildon.

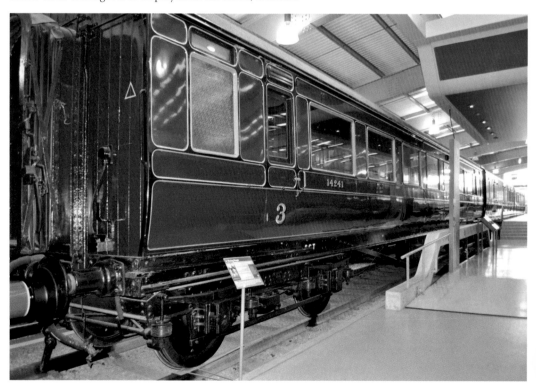

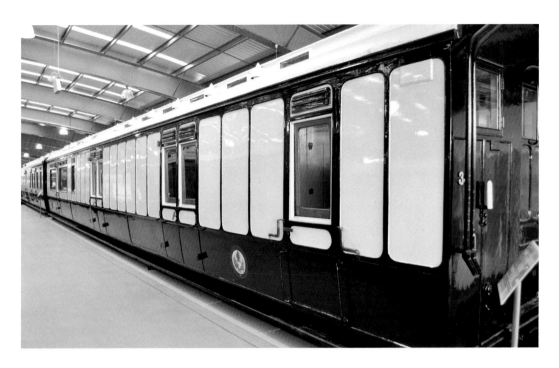

Royal coaches

Royal Escort Car No. 5155 was built at the LNWR's Wolverhampton Works in 1905. Its main purpose was as a 'servants' hall' with accommodation for the royal attendants and the luggage. It continued in use with the LMS, retaining the old milky white and plum livery, and operated as part of the royal train for George V, Edward VIII and Queen Elizabeth II. Below, detail of LNWR Royal Diner Car No. 76 built in 1900, wearing the later LMS badge. Both of these coaches are in the Station Hall at the NRM, York.

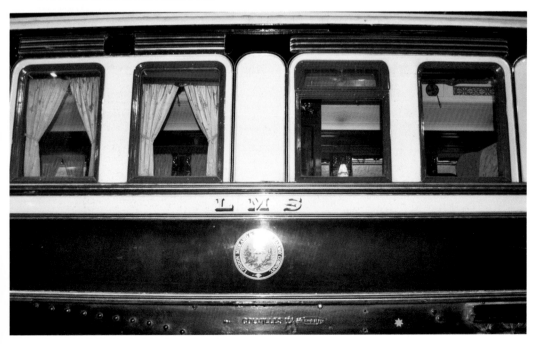

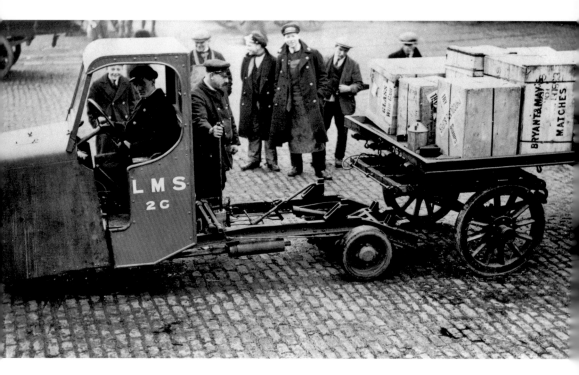

LMS workhorses

The mechanical horse was meant to be a more efficient replacement for some of the hundreds of horses used by the railway company. This is a Karrier Kob Mechanical Horse from the 1930s and in the upper photograph it is shown hitching up to a converted horse-drawn cart. (*CmcC*) This preserved example, below, is at the NRM in York.

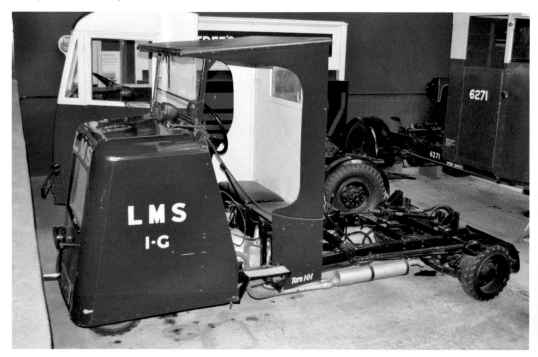

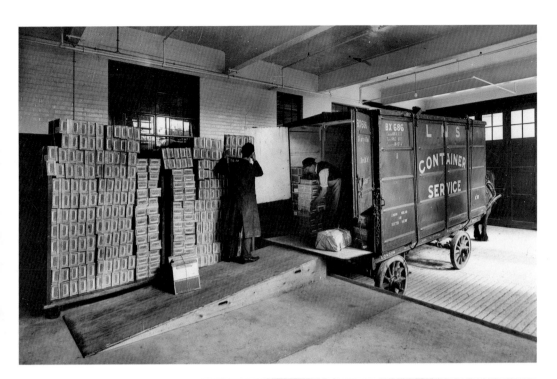

Two more examples of
LMS vehicles. In the
upper photograph an LMS
Type B Container is being
loaded with Barratts Boots
– note the horse waiting
patiently at the front.
Right, photographed at
an unknown location but
possibly Camden, these
Walker six-wheeler 6-ton
mobile cranes were used
by the LMS in larger
goods yards. (*CMcC*)

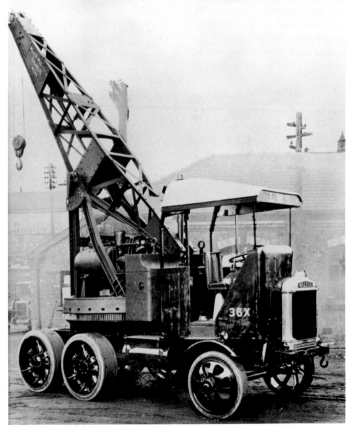

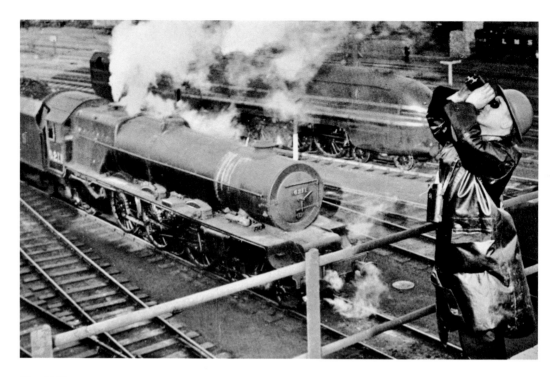

The LMS goes to war

Images from the Second World War: A rooftop spotter scans the sky for enemy aircraft as No. 6211, the Princess Royal Class *Queen Maude*, and an unidentified streamliner pass by. In 1939, special trains also took thousands of schoolchildren away from the cities – the LMS alone transported a quarter of a million evacuees out of London in just four days.

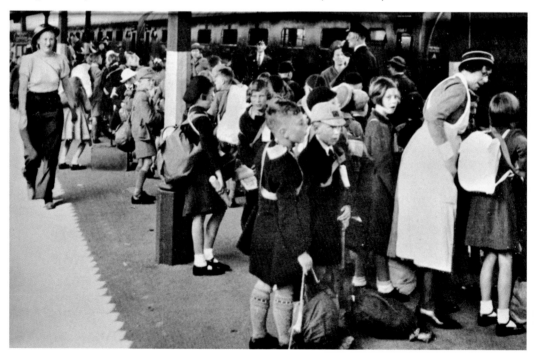

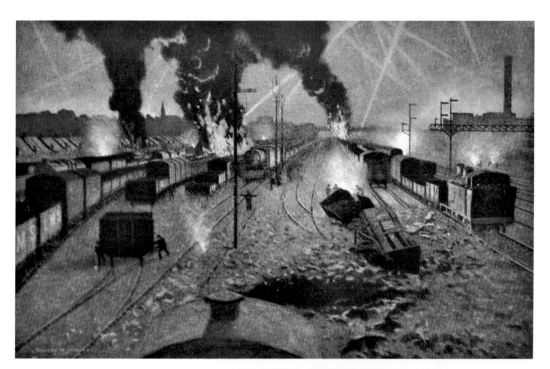

During the war the railway
network attracted frequent
attacks and this illustration
by Norman Wilkinson, taken
from *The LMS at War*, depicts
a raid on the marshalling
yards near Willesden during
the Blitz of September 1940.
Shown right, day in and day
out the company's main line
trains were swamped with
servicemen on the move.

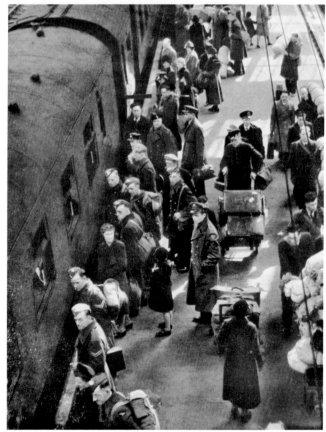

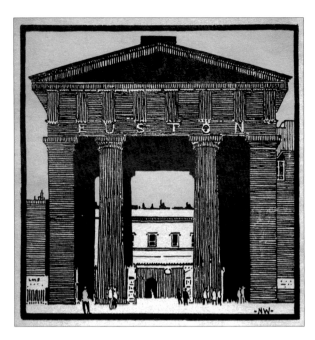 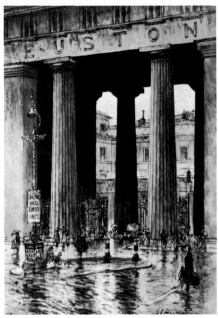

Arch enemies

As an instantly recognised symbol for the station and for the LMS, the Euston Arch was frequently featured in the company's publicity material and publications. It is shown here on the cover of the LMS Route Book, *The Track of the Royal Scot*, and in a 1947 illustration by E. B. Musman.

But behind the scene, some LMS executives harboured plans to replace the old Euston with flashy new headquarters along the lines of the American railroad companies. The reconstruction was announced in 1935 and this illustration depicts one of the proposed schemes – note the LNWR war memorial visible as a dark silhouette. Luckily, the war kept the wrecking balls at bay.

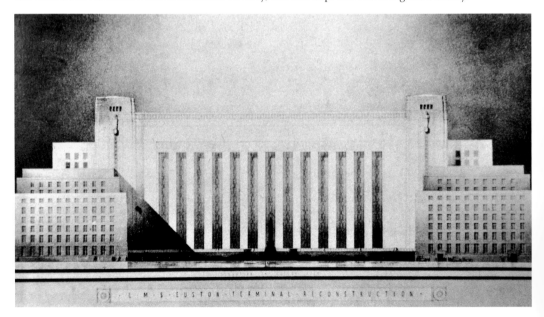

The New Euston

If the past is another place, then the 1960s can be viewed as the place where the future was on offer. It was a time when the post-war greyness of the 1950s was being cast aside and we were promised a future bright with colour television, supersonic air travel, space flight and modern cities with high-rise living. As for the Victorian railways, they were decidedly last century. Their nationalisation and the formation of British Railways in 1948 promised to breathe new life into them. Accordingly, the old familiar company badges gave way to a series of unifying national logos. At first British Railways had the 'cycling lion' crest, then from 1956 the red lion known as the 'ferret and dartboard' and, finally, British Rail's much derided corporate 'arrows of indecision'. Throughout the 1950s and 1960s, passenger numbers were in steady decline as car ownership and road transport increased. The railways were losing money and, in a bid to stem the tide, one third of the network was 're-shaped' by Beeching's axe.

The key to salvaging the railways lay in modernisation. For BR's London Midland Region, this meant the electrification of the West Coast Main Line plus a brand new Euston Station. The challenge, said BR, was to 'produce a new station bold in design and layout and in keeping with a new railway era. As a result, an imaginative and distinctive design has been produced making the station the most modern rail terminal to be found anywhere.' The most controversial part of their plan was the demolition of the Euston Arch along with all of the old station buildings, including the Great Hall, to provide greater space. So what did we get in their place? Here's what British Rail said in *The New Euston Station 1968*, a publication to mark the opening of the station by the Queen on 14 October 1968:

> Simplicity is the keynote in the design of the new Euston. The aim has been to confine all vehicles, mail and parcels to certain areas to give passengers unrestricted movement in the station precincts. At the same time, all the usual amenities and facilities of a modern rail terminal and some new ones too, have been grouped together within easy reach of the travelling public.

This was achieved by creating a modern box of a building, something between an airport terminal and a bus station. The main concourse, covering an area of 30,000 sq feet, was an open two-storey space designed to accommodate the peak time crowds without over-crowding. In theory the concourse walls were entirely glazed, although in practice many of these glass panels led into other station areas, including retail

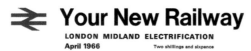

Your New Railway

LONDON MIDLAND ELECTRIFICATION

April 1966   Two shillings and sixpence

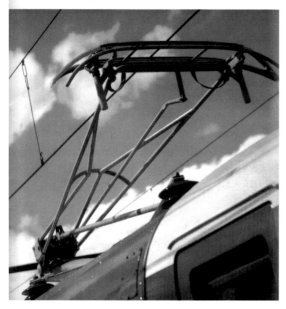

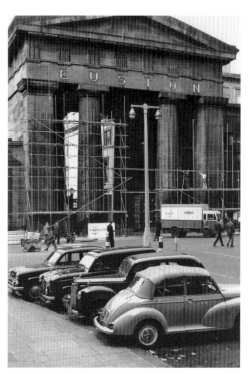

Out with the old ...

The real impetus to rebuild Euston came with the decision to electrify the West Coast Main Line, as the old station couldn't accommodate the wires and gantries. In 1961, the scaffolding went up around the arch so that the demolition team could get to work. Its destruction was brutal and carried out in such a way as to ensure that it could not be rescued. An architect's model, below, shows the layout of the new station with the entrance and main concourse on the left, ramps leading down to the platforms, and the upper storey for the parcel depot and access ramps to the right.

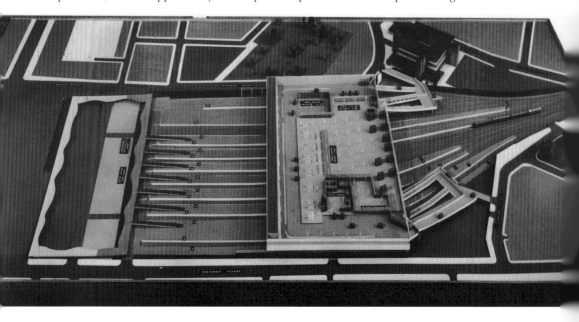

and food outlets. The Travel Centre was located at the western end of the concourse with its booking and reservation facilities beneath a fine 'egg-box' ceiling. Nowadays the concourse area is surprisingly gloomy, even on a sunny day, and the once-bright concrete ceiling has discoloured with time. On the northern side of the concourse there was an airport-style 'electro-mechanically' operated train indicator (now purely electronic) and beneath this a wide letterbox-shaped opening leading to long ramps going down to the platforms themselves.

One aspect where the layout has succeeded is in keeping the travellers and traffic separated. Taxis enter the station from the west side and set down their passengers at basement level. Commercial vehicles enter by way of a service basement road and ramps lead up to the Red Star parcel depot situated on a second storey above the platforms.

So what's not to like? At the time of its rebuilding there was widespread condemnation of the demolition of the old buildings, in particular the Euston Arch. *The Architectural Review* of April 1962 referred to it as the 'Euston Murder' and described its destruction as 'wanton and unnecessary'. And how should we view the new Euston Station today? Writing in *The Times* in 2007, Richard Morrison stated that 'even by the bleak standards of Sixties architecture, Euston is one of the nastiest concrete boxes in London: devoid of any decorative merit, seemingly concocted to induce maximum angst among passengers; and a blight on surrounding streets.'

Seen from our modern perspective, a place where we have come to appreciate London's Victorian stations as important pieces of architecture, as our heritage, it is easy to mock the modernisers of the 1960s. We have learned to value old buildings – even the Victorian ones – we protect them and have devised ways of marrying the old with the new to extend their use and even enhance them. Just take a look at St Pancras or Kings Cross. I enjoy architecture of all sorts and I always try to keep an open mind when assessing a building, seeking those elements that might make it a good example in the context of its times. But even I have to admit that alone among London's railway stations, Euston fails to present any redeeming features. I have absolutely no hesitation in calling for its demolition, which as it turns out, might be exactly what happens when the new HS2 rail link comes to town. Furthermore, we might even see the reconstruction of Euston's iconic arch. Here's hoping.

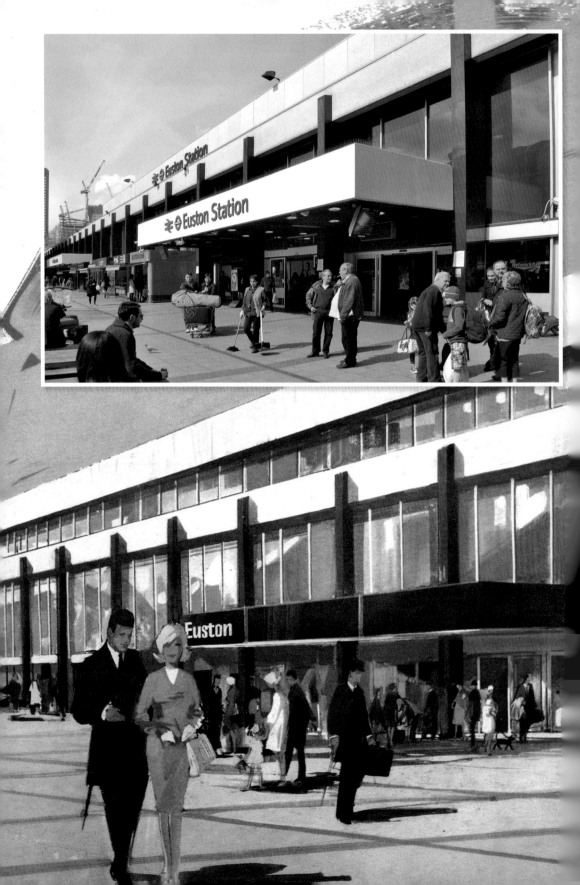

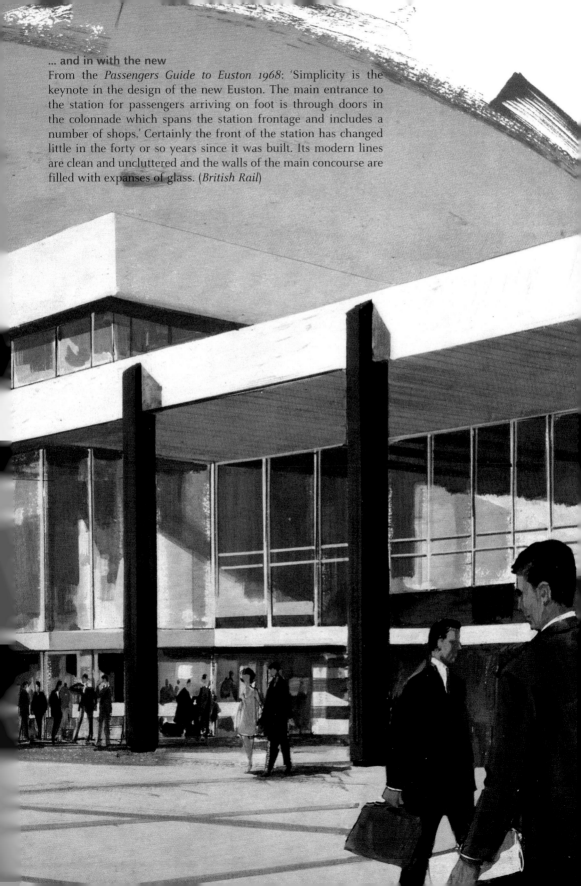

... and in with the new

From the *Passengers Guide to Euston 1968*: 'Simplicity is the keynote in the design of the new Euston. The main entrance to the station for passengers arriving on foot is through doors in the colonnade which spans the station frontage and includes a number of shops.' Certainly the front of the station has changed little in the forty or so years since it was built. Its modern lines are clean and uncluttered and the walls of the main concourse are filled with expanses of glass. (*British Rail*)

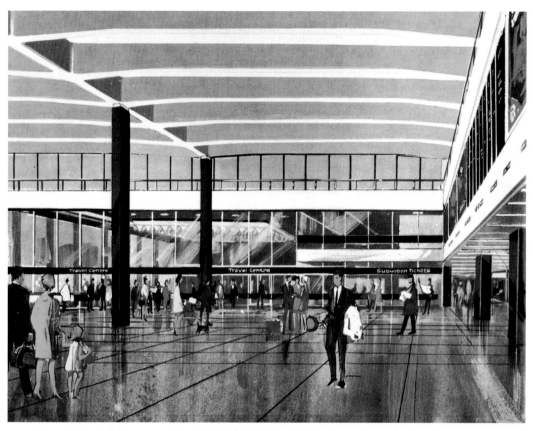

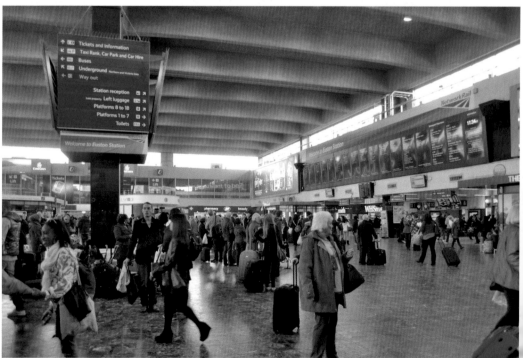

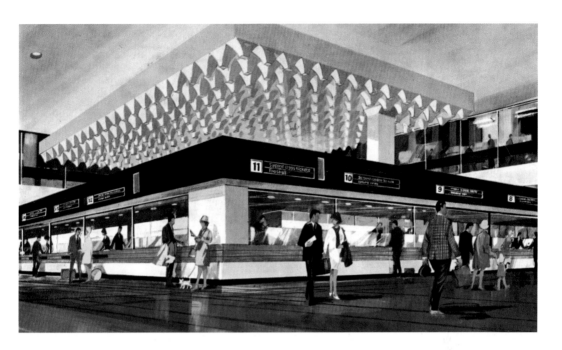

The main concourse

Inside, the building has all the charm of a provincial bus station. The daylight can't get through and the discoloured concrete roof bears down like a heavy overcast. The Travel Centre, situated on the western side of the concourse area, has been restyled and only the 1960s egg-box ceiling remains as a period gem. The electro-mechanical train indicator was an innovation in its time, although this has since been superseded by an electronic version. But as Betjeman observed, unless you want to eat the concourse has nowhere to sit and wait for your train, nowhere to meet family or friends. (*British Rail*)

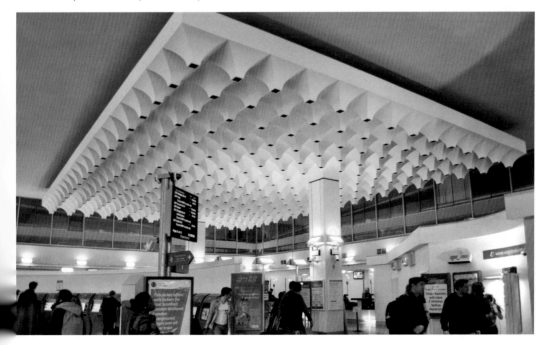

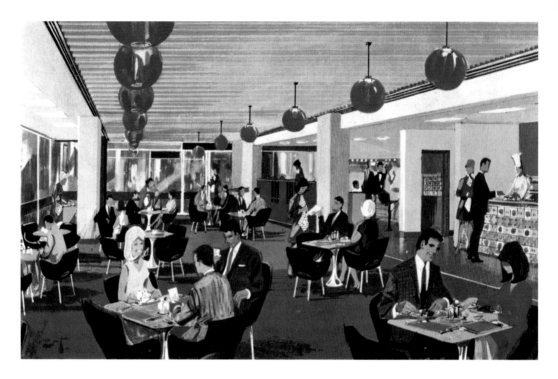

Comfort and convenience

The bright, cheery buffets and grill rooms of the artist's impressions were woefully inadequate for the numbers of real passengers who now pour through the station. They have given way to a plethora of franchises and outlets offering fast food for the fast-moving generation. The original plan had been to offer the 'comfort and convenience of a first class hotel' with first-floor facilities including a waiting lounge with high-class toilets, even showers and baths. (*British Rail*)

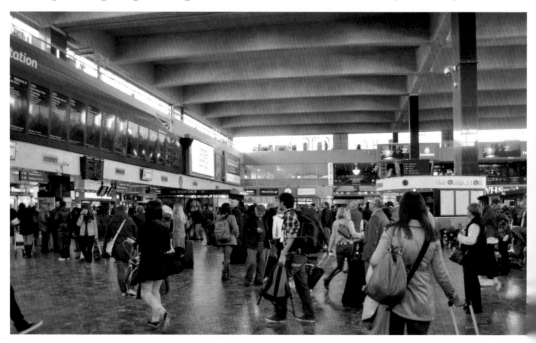

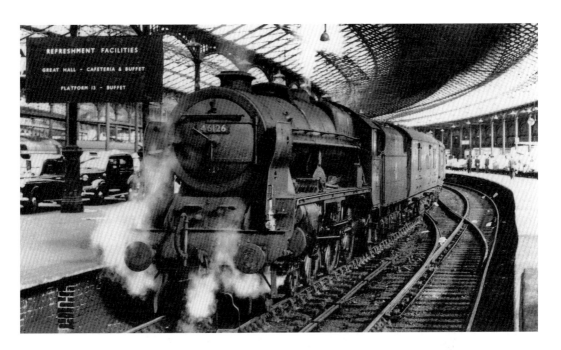

Lost tracks

The rebuilding obliterated all references to Euston's past. In the upper photograph from 1962 a steam loco, the former LMS Royal Scot Class *Royal Army Service Corps*, pulls in at Platform 1. But a year later, this British Rail publicity photo shows a bulldozer getting to work on the old platforms. 'Construction of piles, pilecaps, footings and service trenches had to contend with a bewildering variety of obstructions.' These included a long-forgotten turntable which was salvaged for the railway museum. (*British Rail*)

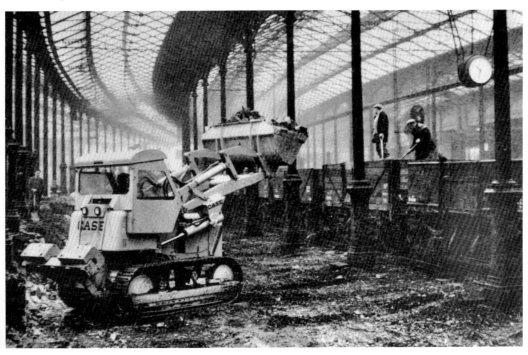

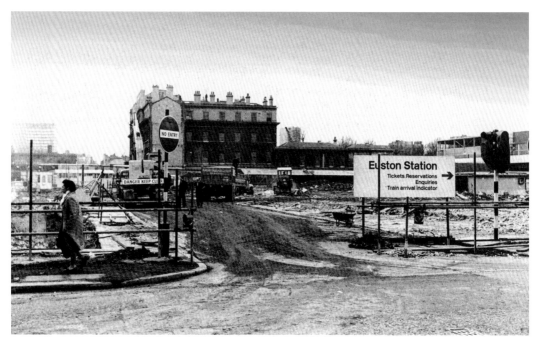

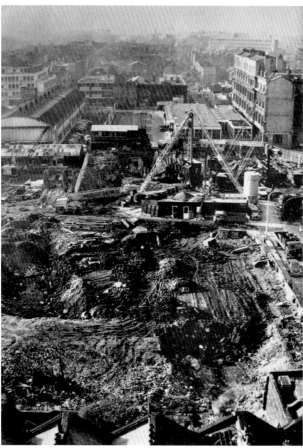

From the ground up
With the buildings and
structures gone, the excavation
work could commence to create
subterranean reception and
departure areas for cars and
taxis. To keep the trains running,
the Birmingham services
were diverted to Paddington
Station while other services
went to either St Pancras or to
Marylebone. (*British Rail*)

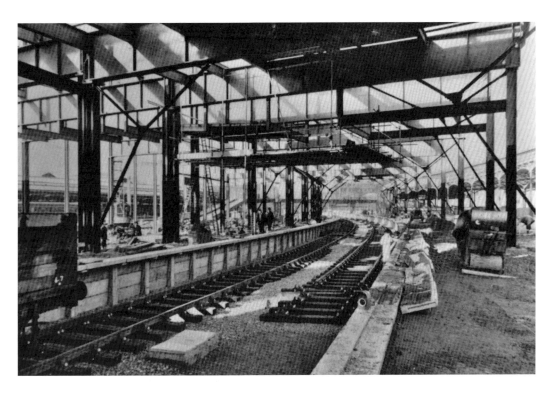

Rebuilding the platforms

The first phase of construction included the eighteen new platforms. With the parcel depot situated above, five-and-a-half thousand tons of structural steelwork were needed to support the parcel deck alone, and pre-stressed concrete units were used to form its floor. Note the raised sections above the track areas to accommodate the overhead cables.

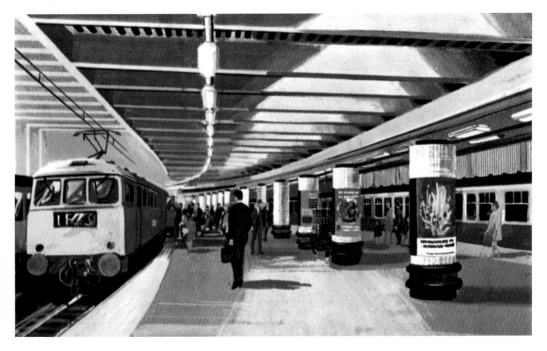

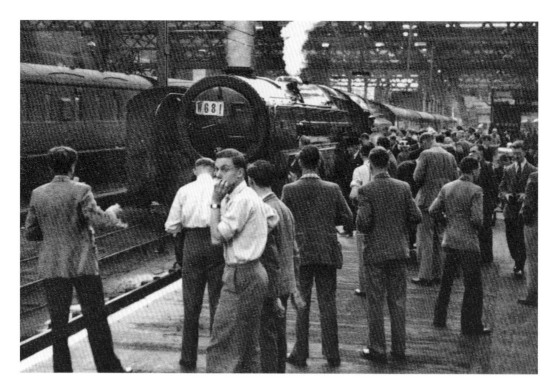

Platforms

A last taste of steam for hundreds of enthusiasts perhaps? A works train departing from the old station. In contrast, we have the present scene, with Platforms 6, 5 and 4, viewed from one of the access slopes leading down from the main concourse, on a quiet Saturday morning.

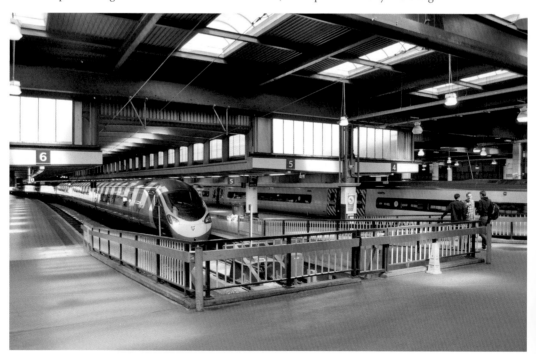

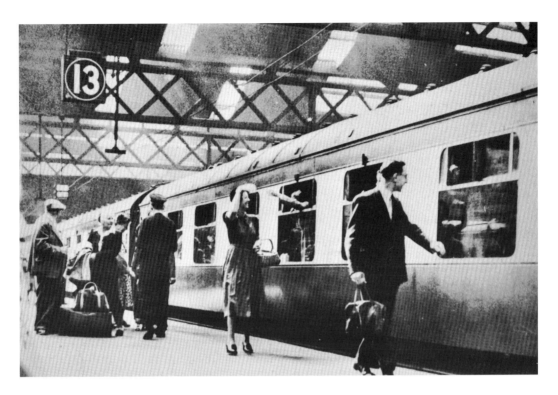

Departures

A train is shown departing from Euston in the final years of the old station in this British Railways photo. Below, a Virgin train waiting to depart from Platform 5 in 2012. Sunlight from the high windows paints the train in these zebra stripes.

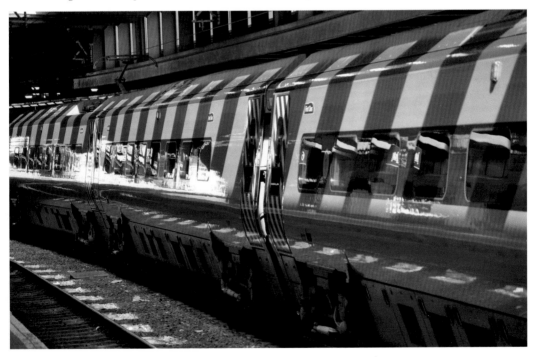

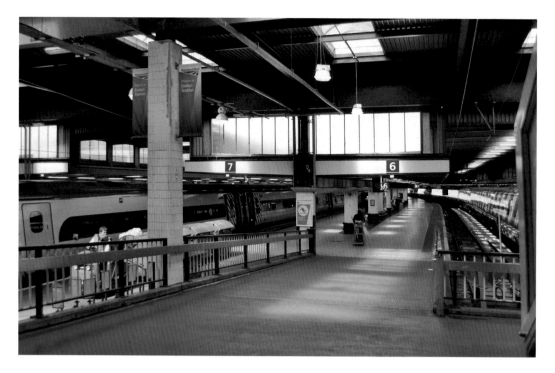

To the trains

Two photographs of the modern Euston. Platforms 7 and 6 in the gloom, above, and the nose of a Virgin Class 390 Pendolino EMU catching the sun to bring a little colour to the otherwise monochromatic scene.

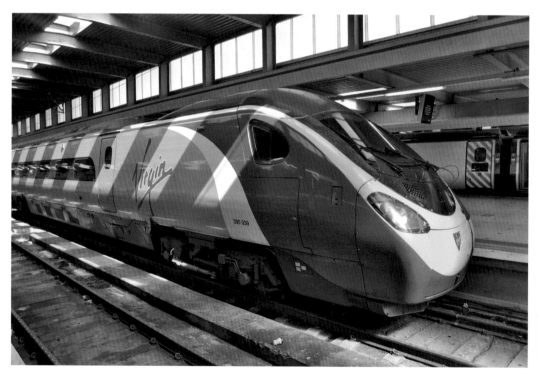

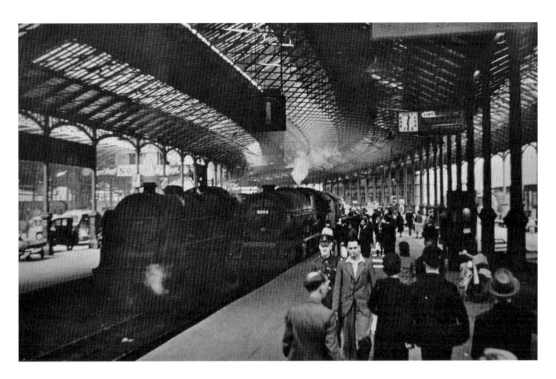

Following the curve

Pre-British Rail steam: No. 6203, the *Princess Margaret Rose*, pulls in to Platform 1, *c.* 1940s. Note the taxis on the cab drive to the left. Below, a Virgin express train on the curves heading northwards out of the gloom.

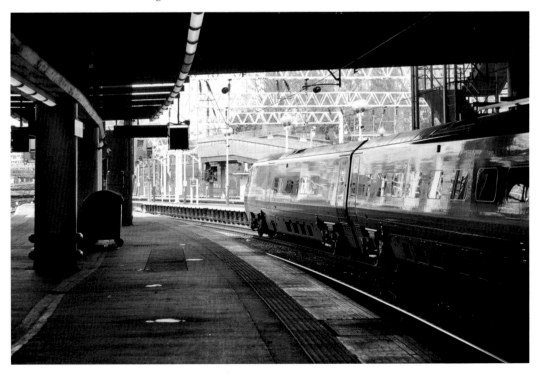

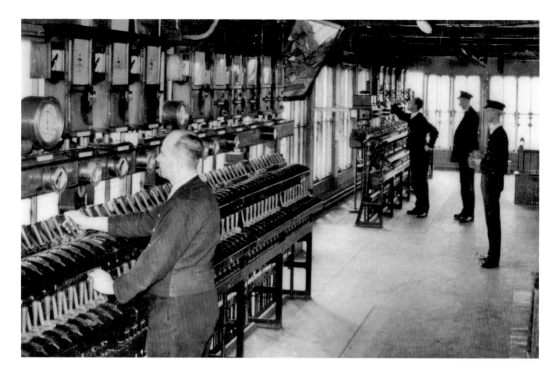

Euston's signal boxes

Above, the interior of an LMS power-operated signal box. In 1952, British Rail opened the new Westinghouse-equipped Euston Power Box to replace three of the station's old signal boxes. The biggest of these, No.1, was built by the LNWR in 1892 and is shown below. The smallest of the old boxes, No.4, survived as the Euston Carriage Sidings Box until the electrification scheme of the 1960s.

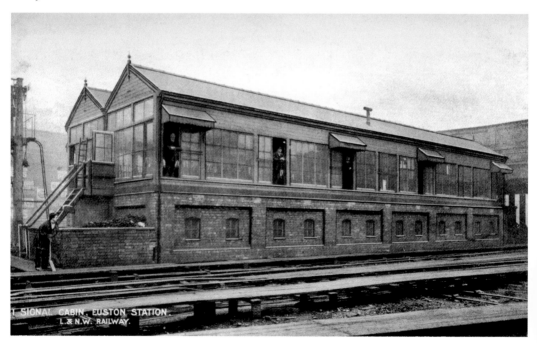

SIGNAL CABIN, EUSTON STATION.
L. & N.W. RAILWAY.

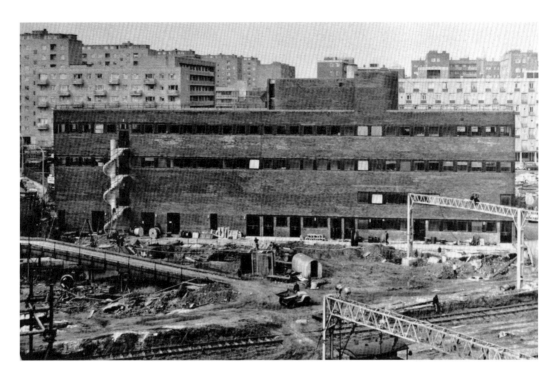

Euston Power Signal Box

From *The New Euston Station 1968*: 'At Euston 2½ route miles, 18 track miles, are controlled from a signal and communications building which was built as part of the new station, replacing four existing signal boxes.' The modern building is on the western side of the tracks, but the Euston PSB closed in 2000 and signalling passed to the Main Line Signalling Control Centre at Wembley.

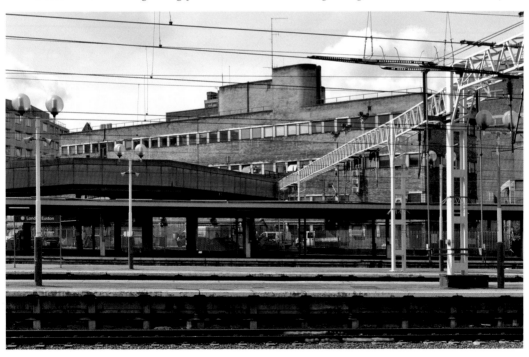

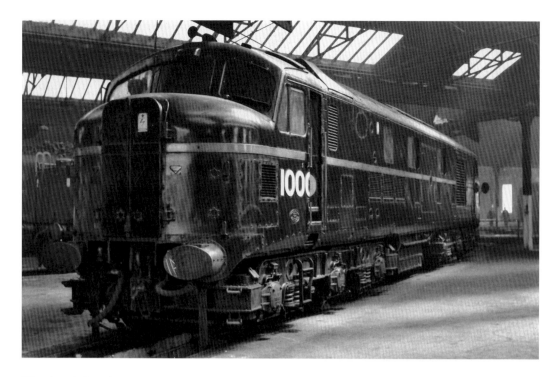

Diesel and electric power

British Rail Class D16/1 No. 10000; together with 10001, these were the first mainline diesels in Britain, built at Derby in 1947 and withdrawn in 1963. The Class 87 Electrics were built between 1972 and 1974 for the new all-electric intercity service to Scotland. Below, No. 87012, *The Olympian*, at Euston. (*Peterdaniel*)

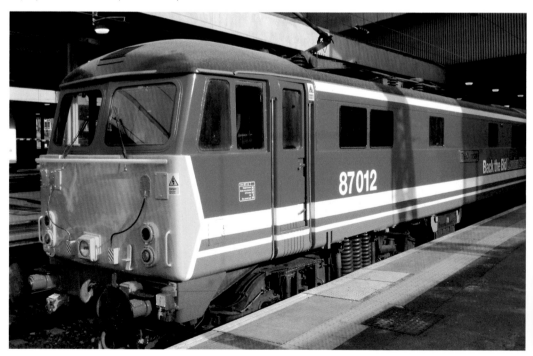

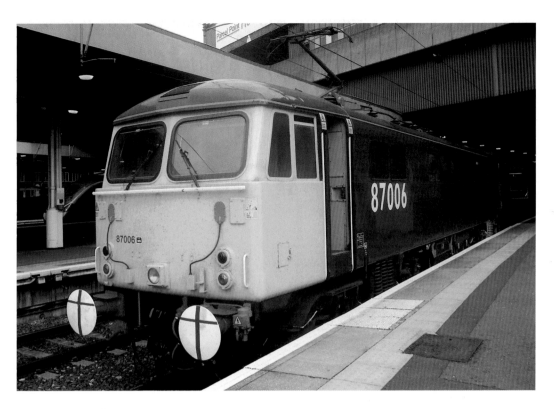

Euston trains

Another Class 87, photographed at Euston Station in 2009. The sign for the Red Star parcel depot is visible on the side of the building. (*Peter Skuse*) Same scene, three years later, with a Virgin Pendolino EMU.

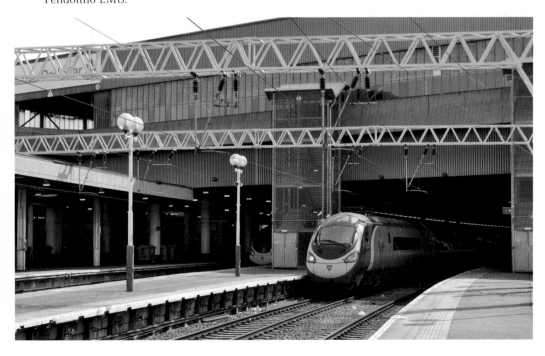

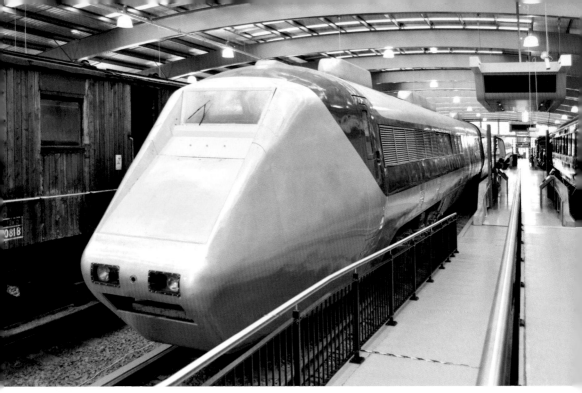

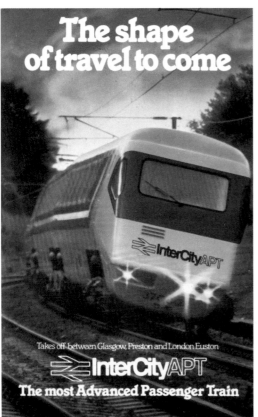

The shape of travel to come

Takes off between Glasgow, Preston and London Euston

InterCity APT

The most Advanced Passenger Train

The shape of travel to come?

The Advanced Passenger Train (APT) was to have been the shape of things to come for the West Coast Main Line. A gas turbine-powered experimental testbed, the APT-E, above, was constructed in 1972 and it led to three electrically-powered prototypes known as British Rail Class 370 APT-Ps. The first public run, from Glasgow to Euston, took place on 7 December 1981, but this was before the bugs in the titling system had been ironed out. Consequently technical and reliability issues, gleefully reported by a critical press, saw the APTs dubbed as the 'Accident Prone Trains' and all three were withdrawn from service by 1986. The experimental APT-E is on display at the NRM in Shildon, County Durham, and APT-P, No. 370 006, is preserved at the Crewe Heritage Centre.

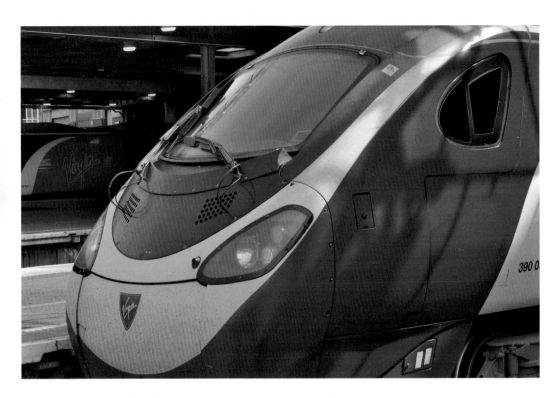

West Coast Main Line

The modern express trains on the WCML, Virgin's fleet of Class 390 Pendolino EMUs were introduced in July 2002. They have a top speed of 140 mph (225 km/h). Shown above at Euston in 2012 and, below, alongside the M1 near Daventry. (*G-Man*)

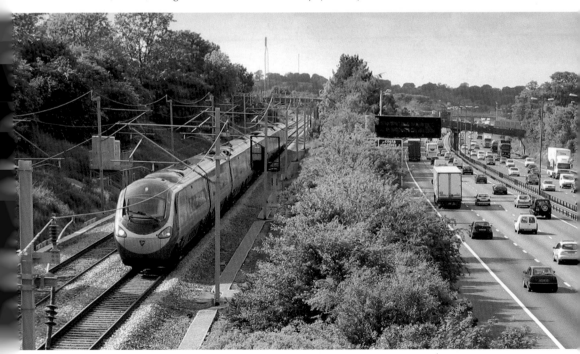

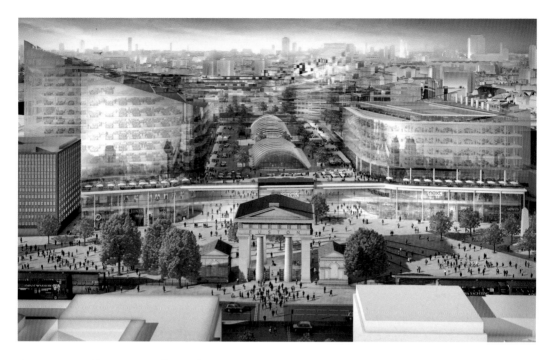

A new Euston for a new train service

Campaigners fighting for the reinstatement of the Euston Arch may get their wish with the announcement of the proposed High-Speed 2 (HS2) rail link between London and Birmingham. Euston has been selected as the London terminus and initial artist impressions of a radical redevelopment feature a restored arch. In this bird's-eye view it is shown in a new position, brought forward from the old one and sited between the two lodges on Euston Street. The lower image shows the new station frontage with the LNWR war memorial remaining in its present position. The corner of the west lodge is glimpsed on the far right. (*HS2*)

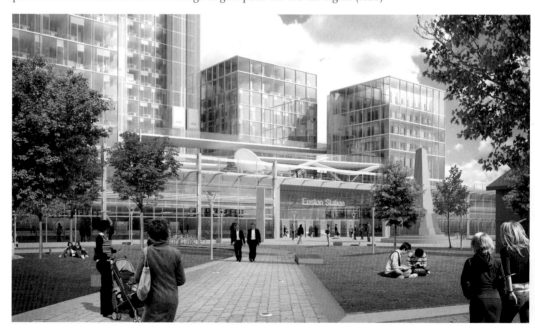

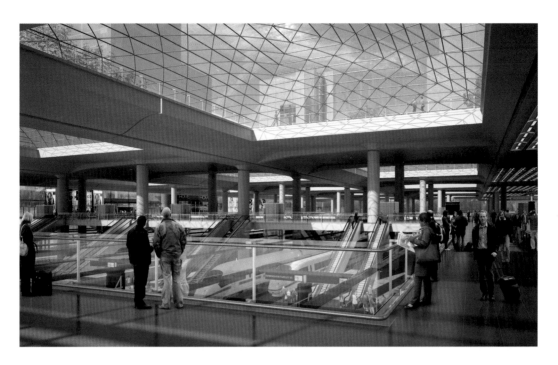

After the gloom of the 1960s concrete, the new station concourse is full of light with the tracks located on a lower level. Below, when the Euston Arch was demolished many of the stones were dumped in the Prescott Channel in the East End. Some stones have now been salvaged. (*Gordon Joly*)

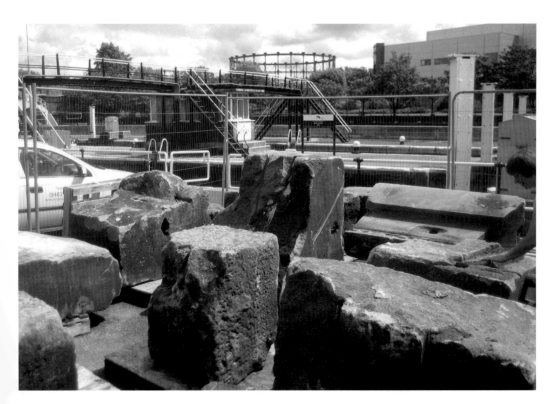

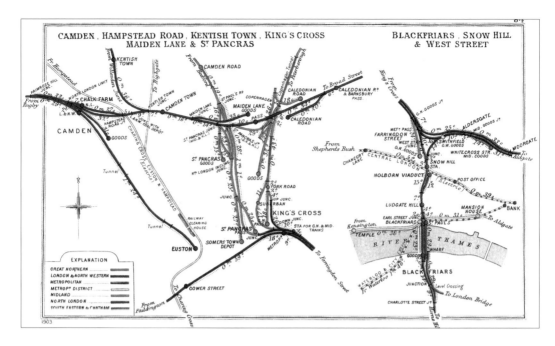

Connections

1903 railway map showing the positions of Euston and the Camden Goods Yard, as well as the proximity of both St Pancras and Kings Cross. Below, each station on the Victoria Line, opened in 1969, features a motif to help the traveller identify their location. Euston has its famous arch.

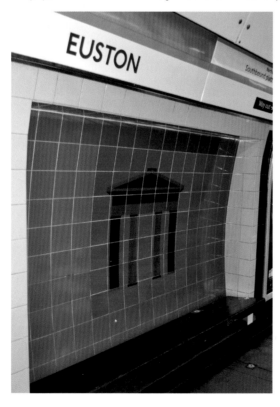

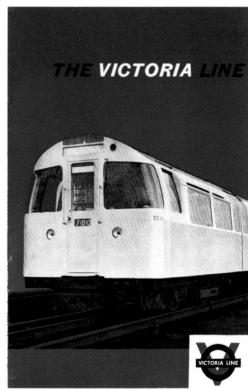

Connections

Euston Station and Euston Square

The London Underground first came to Euston Station in May 1907 when the City & South London Railway (C&SLR) opened a station on Eversholt Street, just to the east of the mainline station. Just over a month later, the Charing Cross, Euston & Hampstead Railway (CCE&HR) opened its station to the west of Euston Station. The building was designed by Leslie Green and finished in the distinctive ox-blood red terracotta tiling he devised for the CCE&HR. The two stations were sufficiently close together that passageways were soon constructed to link them to each other and, via lifts, the mainline station. With no need for three entrances, the two station buildings were closed. The C&SLR and CCE&HR stations came under the joint ownership of the Underground Group in 1913 and various improvements were made in the 1920s. In 1967, the Victoria Line was opened to ease congestion on existing underground services, and a ticket hall was constructed below the newly built Euston Station concourse.

Euston is not on the Circle Line, although the nearby Euston Square Station, on the south side of Euston Street, is served by the Circle, Hammersmith & City and Metropolitan lines. A new entrance has been created in the corner of the Wellcome Trust building in Gower Street to replace the original one. There is also a subway entrance on the north side of Euston Street. Network Rail has announced plans to create a further subway link to connect the mainline station with Euston Square.

The Euston Bus Station is located beneath the office buildings in front of the railway station.

Camden

Opened in 1907, Camden Town tube station began life as part of the CCE&HR and it is where the line branches into two for Hampstead and Highgate. Another of Leslie Green's designs, this is said to be one of the busiest underground stations in London because of the tourists who pour into Camden at weekends, to the extent that entry is restricted on Sundays. Transport for London has applied to completely rebuild the station, but permission was declined in 2005. Further up Camden Road is the Chalk Farm tube station, the nearest one to the Camden Roundhouse and former railway yard buildings, located on the junction of Chalk Farm Road, Haverstock Hill and Adelaide Road. It also opened in 1907, designed by Green once again, and is now on the Edgware branch of the Northern Line.

Camden Road Station is a former Midland Railway station on the main line to St Pancras and has no direct link to Euston Station.

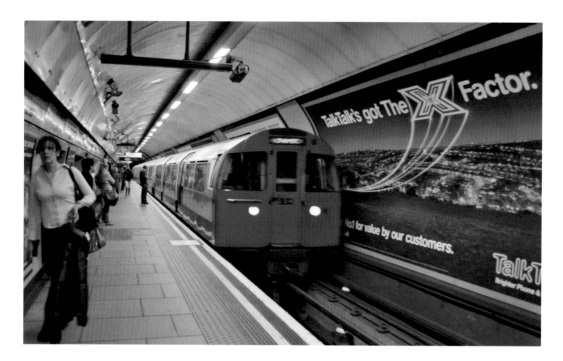

Underground Euston
Original 1967 'C' stock on the Victoria Line in 2011. Below, Euston Square Station on the south side of Euston Road. The original station is around the corner and was originally known as Gower Street. This new entrance in the corner of the Wellcome Trust building opened in 2011. (*Ewan Munro*)

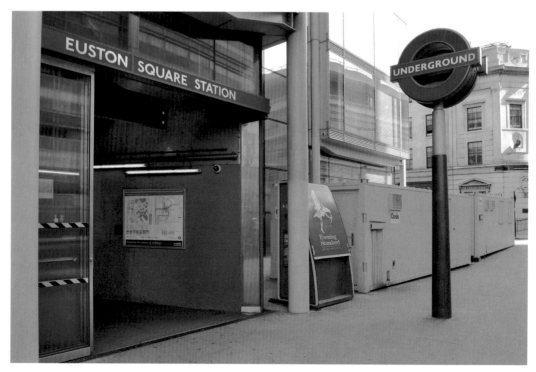

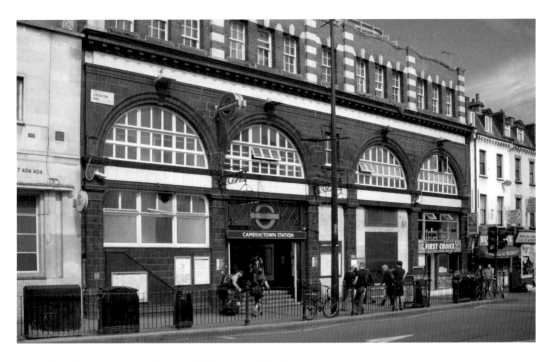

The Charing Cross, Euston & Hampstead Railway

The CCE&HR underground stations at Camden Town and Chalk Farm were designed by architect Leslie Green and feature distinctive ox-blood coloured tiles, horizontal banding and half-circle windows. Badly damaged in the Blitz, Camden Town is now one of the busiest stations on the Underground. (*Amy in Holland*) Chalk Farm, just up the road, has the longest frontage of any of Green's buildings. They are both served by the Northern Line.

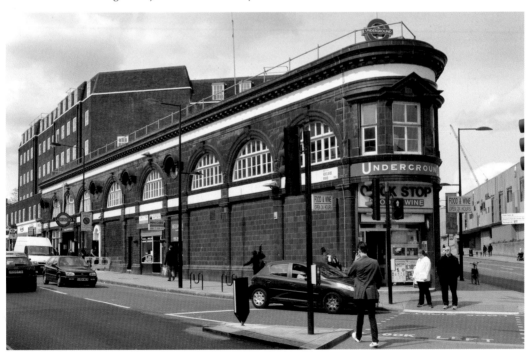

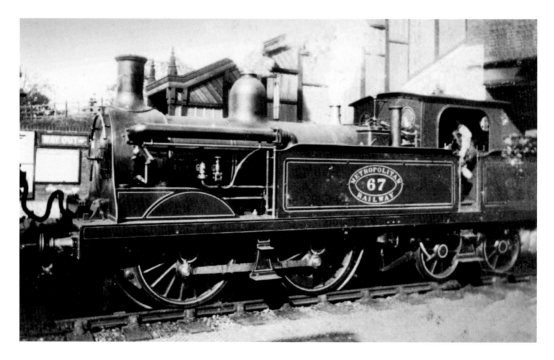

Metropolitan steam

The Metropolitan Railway was the first underground line in London when it opened in 1863, and it is also one of the shallowest lines, built by the cut-and-cover method. Above, No. 67, an 0-4-4T locomotive with condensers. Below the preserved Metropolitan No. 23 at the TfL London Transport Museum, Covent Garden.

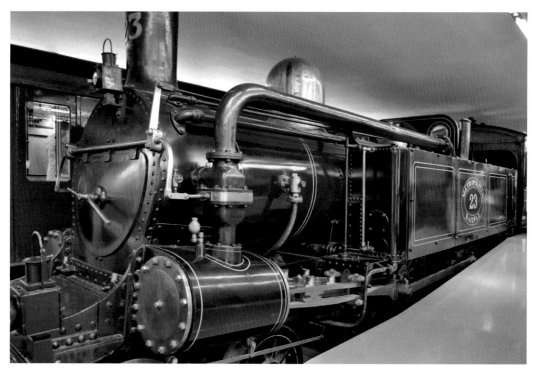

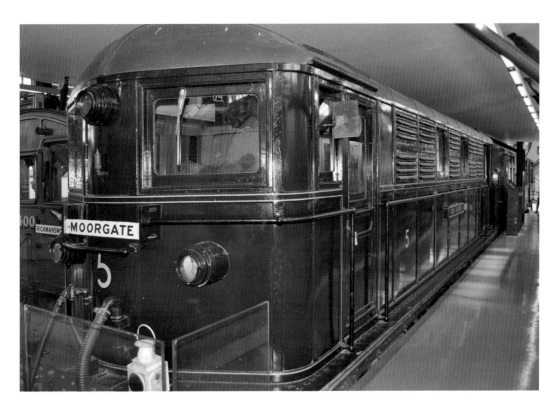

Electric underground

Electrification of the trains solved the problem of smoke and steam underground. Two Metropolitan Vickers Electric locomotives: Above, No. 5 which is displayed at the LTM in Covent Garden, and below, a contemporary photograph of No. 10, the *William Ewart Gladstone*.

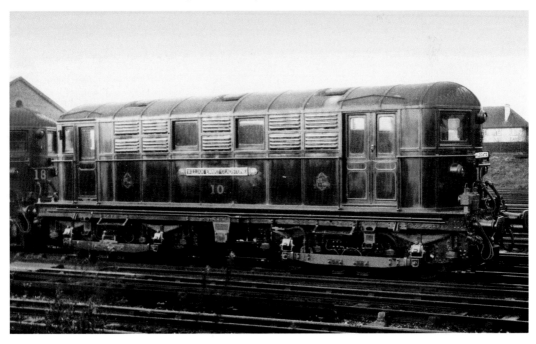

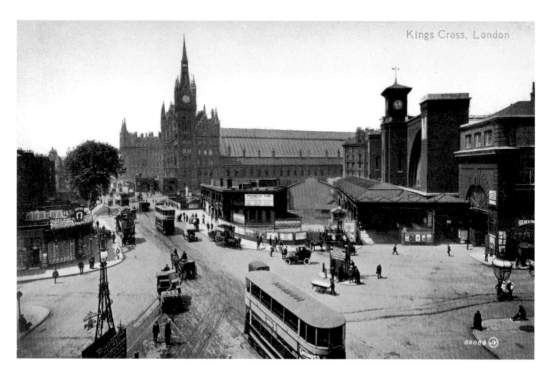

Close neighbours
Because Parliament did not allow the railways to penetrate any further into the city, Euston Road is scattered with the termini for a number of companies. To the east of Euston, the spire of the Midland Railway Hotel at St Pancras looks down on the older Kings Cross.

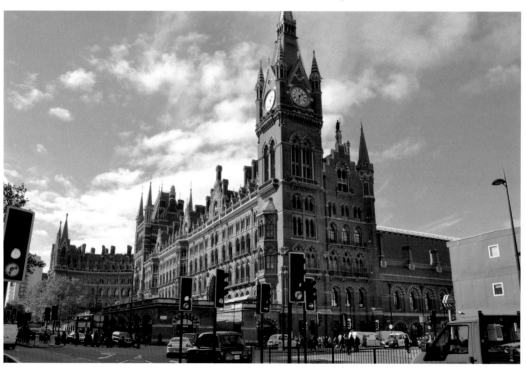

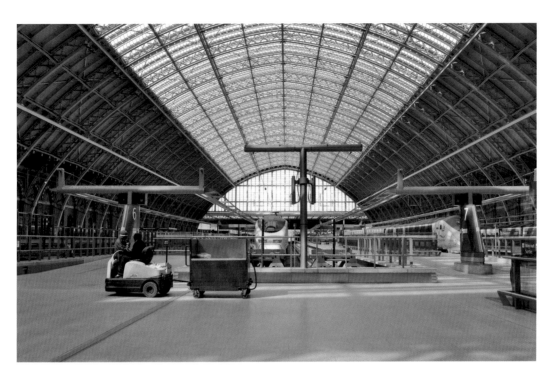

St Pancras train shed

Unbelievably, St Pancras was nearly demolished at one time as it was no longer needed. Now the Eurostar service and a major refurbishment have given new life to Barlow's stunning single-span train shed.

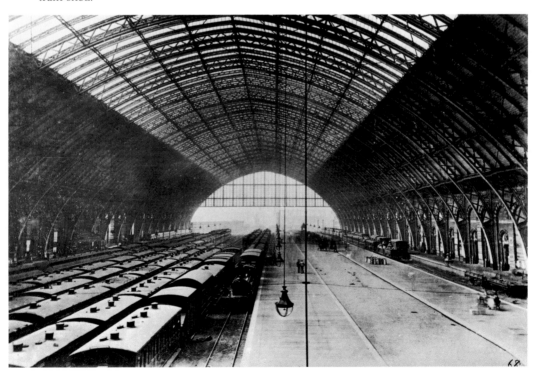

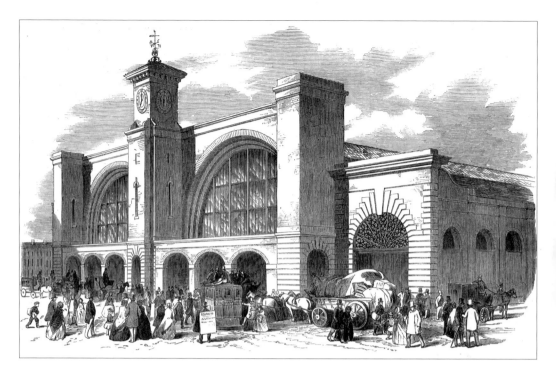

Kings Cross

Like the ugly duckling, the twin-roofed train shed at Kings Cross has also been given a long overdue makeover. It has been de-cluttered, the roof refurbished to let the light pour in, and station access has been improved with a new footbridge and lifts. More drastically, a new concourse has been created with a sculptural roof that links the old station building to the curved front of the Kings Cross Hotel.

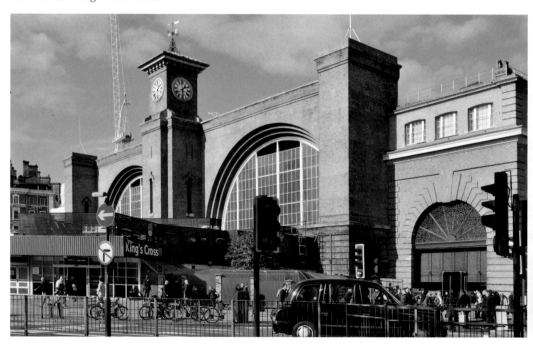

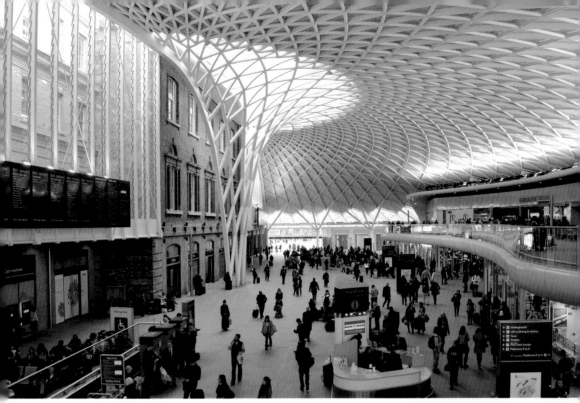

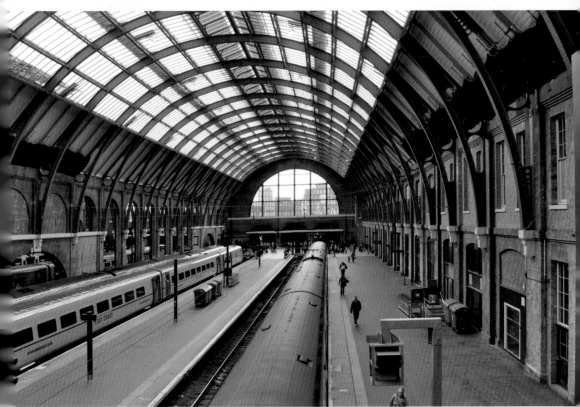

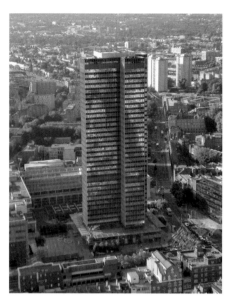

The two towers

In keeping with the drive for modernity at Euston Station, the area has two towers which were also started in the 1960s. Euston Tower, above, is a thirty-six floor skyscraper completed in 1970. It is 407 feet (124 m) high. (*James Cridland*) Considerably taller at 581 feet (177 m), the BT Tower, as the Post Office Tower is now known, has become such an iconic landmark on the city skyline that it was granted Grade II listed status in 2003. Completed in May 1966, it was the tallest structure in London for many years. The famous revolving restaurant at the top was operated by the Butlins organisation, but closed in 1980 for security reasons. (*David Castor/KC2000*)

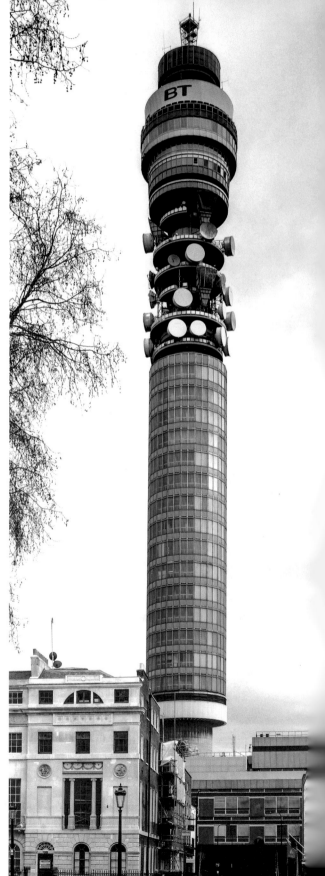

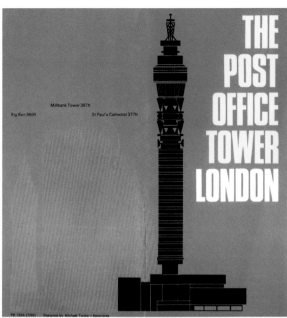

THE POST OFFICE TOWER LONDON

Millbank Tower 387ft
Big Ben 360ft
St Paul's Cathedral 377ft

PH 1594 (7/66)   Designed by Michael Tucker Associates

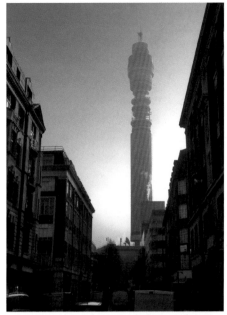

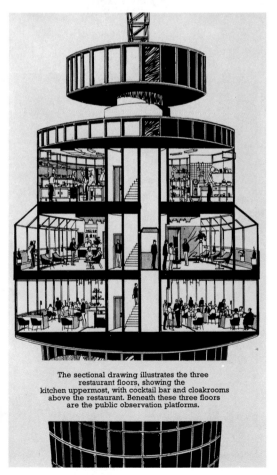

The sectional drawing illustrates the three restaurant floors, showing the kitchen uppermost, with cocktail bar and cloakrooms above the restaurant. Beneath these three floors are the public observation platforms.

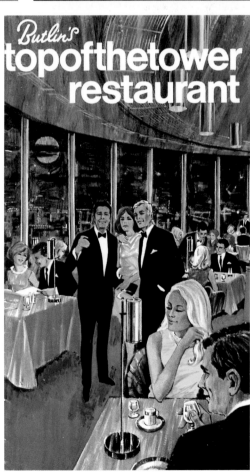

Butlin's topofthetower restaurant

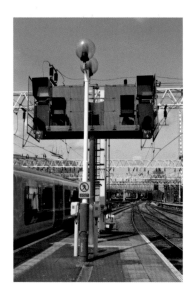

The end of Platforms 7 and 6, Euston Station, 2012.

Further reading

A Century of Progress – London-Birmingham 1838–1938, LMS, 1938.

London Historic Railway Stations, by John Betjeman, John Murray, 1978.

The New Euston Station 1968, British Rail, 1968.

The Euston Arch and the Growth of the London, Midland & Scottish Railway, by Alison and
    Peter Smithson, Thames & Hudson, 1968.

Online resources

The Euston Arch Trust – www.eustonarch.org

Network Rail information – www.networkrail.co.uk/Euston.aspx

LNWR Society – www.lnwrs.org.uk

LMS Society – www.lmssociety.org.uk

Camden Railway Heritage Trust – www.crht1837.org

Acknowledgements

I would like to acknowledge and thank the many individuals and organisations who have
contributed to the production of this book. In particular, Campbell McCutcheon of Amberley
Publishing for commissioning this Through Time series on London's railway termini.

Unless otherwise stated, all new photography is by the author. Additional images have
come from a number of sources and I am grateful to the following: Peter James, Tivedshambo,
Peter Skuse, Peterdaniel, Gordon Joly, G-Man, Ewan Munro, Amy in Holland, David Castor,
KC2000, James Cridland, the US Library of Congress (LoC), Campbell McCutcheon (CMcC),
HS2, British Rail, Network Rail, and the Nanyang Technological University (NTU).

Final thanks go to my wife, Ute Christopher, who assisted with proof reading. Apologies
to anyone left out unknowingly and any such errors brought to my attention will be
corrected in subsequent editions. JC